"The coach's tips are very helpful—advice from a pro. Paul's book will help you spot trouble areas that you can fix or avoid and help you focus on what you have to offer to land the job."

MARJORIE BLANCHARD, PH.D.
President
Blanchard Training & Development, Inc.

❋

"A treasure-trove of real-life examples, practical tips, and useful exercises that will prepare you for your next interview—and the rest of your life. Invest in yourself. Get and study *Get Hired!* "

JIM KOUZES
Coauthor of *The Leadership Challenge* and *Credibility*
Chairman and CEO
Tom Peters Group/Learning Systems

❋

"Paul Green is one of the world's leading experts on interviewing. Packed with great content, his new book is worth far more than the price. Everyone would be a big winner if companies would give a copy to all their job candidates."

ARTHUR R. BAUER
President
American Media Inc.
Producer of *More Than a Gut Feeling*

❋

"*Get Hired!* does a great job of helping people prepare for the interview. It provides a comprehensive understanding of the interviewer's job—and with this information, a job candidate can size up an interview situation and successfully handle various interview approaches."

LEN SCHLESINGER
Professor
Harvard Business School

GET HIRED!
WINNING
STRATEGIES
TO ACE THE
INTERVIEW

GET HIRED!

WINNING STRATEGIES TO ACE THE INTERVIEW

Paul C. Green, Ph.D.

BARD PRESS
Austin, Texas

GET HIRED!
WINNING STRATEGIES TO ACE THE INTERVIEW

Bard Press
Suite 205
1515 Capital of Texas Highway South
Austin, Texas 78746
Phone: (512) 329-8373   Fax (512) 329-6051

Behavioral Technology®, Inc.
6260 Poplar Avenue
Memphis, TN 38119-4719
Phone (800) 227-6855 Fax (901) 763-3637
BeTech@ix.netcom.com

ORDERING INFORMATION

To order additional copies, contact your local bookstore or call **(800) 227-6855**. Quantity discounts are available.

ISBN trade paperback 1-885167-14-8
ISBN hardcover 1-885167-13-X

Library of Congress Cataloging-in-Publication Data
Green, Paul C.
    Get hired : winning strategies to ace the interview / Paul C. Green.
       p.   cm.
    Includes bibliographical references and index.
    ISBN 1-885167-13-X. — ISBN 1-885167-14-8 (pbk.)
    1. Employment interviewing—Handbooks, manuals, etc. 2. Job hunting—Handbooks, manuals, etc.   I. Title.
    HF5549.5.I6G74   1996
    650.1'4—dc20   96-4781
                                                  CIP

CREDITS

Production manager: Sherry Sprague
Developmental editor: Jeff Morris
Copyeditor: Deborah Costenbader
Proofreaders: Laurie Drummond, Doreen Piano, Virginia Watkins
Cover and text design: Steve Lux Design
Cover photography: Marshall Harrington Photography
Index: Linda Webster

First printing, May 1996
Second printing, October 1996

TABLE OF CONTENTS

ABOUT THE AUTHOR

Dr. Paul C. Green, an industrial organizational psychologist, has over twenty-five years of experience in corporate training and consulting. As founder and CEO of Behavioral Technology®, Inc., Dr. Green has focused his professional interest on helping companies enhance their human resource selection and development systems. He has personally conducted over five thousand selection interviews with a wide variety of Fortune 100 organizations. In addition, he has conducted over one thousand Behavioral Interviewing® workshops, training an estimated 150,000 managers in behavioral-based interviewing throughout North America.

Dr. Green earned his Ph.D. in industrial organizational psychology from the University of Memphis in 1970. Based on his research and practical experience, he developed the Behavioral Interviewing training program. This instructional approach stresses the importance of using past behavior as a predictor of future job performance. Dr. Green and his associates have interviewed candidates and trained managers for such organizations as Federal Express, Hewlett-Packard, Intel, Covey Leadership Center, Motorola, EDS, Harley Davidson, the Department of Defense, and the Internal Revenue Service. He has authored numerous papers and films, including *More Than a Gut Feeling*, the world's best-selling interview training video.

ACKNOWLEDGMENTS

This book is the product of the skill and effort of many people.

First I must acknowledge the many clients I have had the privilege of working with. It was their experiences, questions, and techniques that I described and explained in this book. They are the ones who really did most of the concept development.

My professional colleagues at Behavioral Technology®, Inc., gave me a most valuable gift: time. They held their questions, solved problems themselves, and most of all, tolerated my putting an "emergencies only" sign on my door. This allowed me to write the book during work hours in a period when our company grew about 50 percent.

The entire Behavioral Technology team, our account consultants, account executives, marketing associates, internal development, and support staff, responded to whatever was needed with speed and style.

Jeff Morris gave me the hands-on guidance, revisions, and savvy that a first-book author needs. He showed me how to focus on what the job candidate would want to know and leave out everything else. He demonstrated tactful persistence in giving me direction and an experienced hand in helping me communicate with readers.

My wife, Jenny, counseled me through my areas of confusion, while expertly sensing when she should keep her distance from a preoccupied writer. She had an astonishing ability to change my perspective and then leave me alone to think.

Thank you all.

Paul C. Green, Ph.D.
Memphis, Tennessee
January 1996

PART ONE

PUT
YOURSELF
IN THE
BIG
PICTURE

Some time ago I got a telephone call from a friend who was very troubled. Now, this is someone I once worked with and have known for years. He was, and still is, a rock-solid guy. In all the time I worked with him I never saw him rattled, even when he was being yelled at by the CEO of his company. But on this day his speech was halting and his voice was shaking. He had just been terminated.

"I got sideways between my boss and the VP of operations," he said. "Not the first time, as you well know, but this time it went against me. I was right, but career-wise I was dead wrong. They didn't fire me right away; they waited a decent interval, then 'downsized' my position. So I'm on the street now, a place I never thought I'd be at my age.

"Fact is, Paul, I don't know what to do. I'll try to round up as many interviews as I can, of course, but I don't think I've got much of a chance. The competition's going to be murder. I'll have to go up against people who still have jobs, and what organization's going to choose a middle-aged middle manager who's been cut loose?

"I know this organization inside out; but that was then and this is now, and I don't know anything else. I've been trying to update my résumé, but I'm having a lot of trouble describing what I know, what I can do. I know I did my part, that I was a major player here, but that's all gone.

"It's a heck of a thing, being sacked after eighteen productive years at one company. I don't even feel like me anymore, Paul. It's like being lost in the desert without water. I never knew I could feel so alone."

It was a story I've heard many times before and many times since—though never from someone I knew so well. I was glad he had called me; I knew I could reassure him.

"I know it feels like it's the end of the world and you're the last person left alive," I told him, "but believe me—you're not alone. The whole world of work is turning upside down. Everybody's changing jobs, and everybody's job is changing. You'd be surprised at how many people are having the same experience. More and more people are changing jobs, even changing careers, instead of staying in one job all their lives. *That's* your competition. They're no better or worse off than you.

"In fact, you may have a distinct advantage over them. I'll tell you why. First of all, you're getting a head start on developing the most important skill you and everybody else will need in the future—marketing your job skills.

"Second, you and I can explore the practical steps you can take to make an effective work search. We can use my experience interviewing thousands of candidates and clearly define what organizations are looking for. That should be enough to help us guide your planning. Together we can anticipate what you're going to run into and how to prepare for tough interviews.

"I'm really glad you called me. You're talking to someone who really wants to help you. It might surprise you to learn there's a well-defined technology behind making an effective work search. I'll help you apply that technology toward getting yourself a good job."

CHAPTER 1

SETTING OUT
ON YOUR JOB
JOURNEY

Because you've opened this book and started reading, I can tell you something about yourself that is probably true:

You're looking for a job.

Maybe you lost your last position in a corporate restructuring and are looking for a new job. Maybe you have a job now but you're thinking of leaving it or you're worried about losing it. Maybe you've been out of the job market for a while and want to get back into it. Maybe you're a high school or college graduate looking for your first job. Or maybe your organization is downsizing and you've been asked to interview in order to keep the job you have.

Whatever your situation, you're probably feeling the stress. One day you're full of courage and optimism, moving inexorably onward and upward toward your career destiny; the next day you're down, worried that you won't get the interview you want, or that the interviewer won't like you, or that you'll blow it and lose your chance at your dream job.

Don't worry—these ups and downs are perfectly normal. A lot of it has to do with the culture you live in—a culture that places enormous value on employment, in which a person's self-esteem, rightly or wrongly, is tied closely to working and being paid for it. When you're out of a job, your self-esteem may start to fall, and if you're unemployed for long, it can plummet out of sight and make it that much harder to get out and look for work.

I will offer two practical tips about feeling this way. First, it's not a disgrace to be out of a job. It's a very common condition these days. The workplace is changing rapidly, and people change jobs more often than they used to. Second, the best way to regain and sustain your confidence and self-esteem is to take action. Action combats anxiety.

You've already taken the first positive step toward correcting your situation: you've started reading this book.

And I'm going to help you **get hired.**

I can say this with some confidence. If you follow the advice I'm giving you in this book, you will dramatically increase your chances of getting a good job—the job that you're best suited for, perhaps even the dream job you've been steering your career toward.

This book will help you learn how to
- manage your feelings in and around interviews
- provide specific, honest information about your skills
- talk about how the employer can benefit by hiring you
- respond to questions about negatives in your skills
- keep your mouth shut on potentially explosive issues
- pick up the pieces when you don't get the job offer

and much more. Along the way I will share with you my twenty-five years of experience interviewing candidates for a wide variety of jobs in both the private sector and government. I will give you practical advice based on over ten years of experience as an outplacement consultant, helping people find new jobs. From my experience in training tens of thousands of managers how to conduct selection interviews, I will explain what you can expect most interviewers to say and do.

WHAT IT'S ALL ABOUT

The focus of *Get Hired!* is the interview. In writing the book, I tried to put myself in your shoes—a job candidate aspiring to do well enough in an interview to get a job offer. The five parts of the book will tell you, in turn, what you will find in today's job market and the four basic kinds of interviewers you can expect to encounter; how to assess yourself and your job skills; how to prepare for the interview; what you can expect during the interview; and what to do after the interview.

GOING THROUGH THE MOTIONS

I was standing in the shopping center watching the crowds go by when I saw a manager I had known several years ago. Smart and well educated, he had been ideally suited for his career, conducting customer surveys and developing market trends for a large multinational company.

His looks had changed. He seemed about an inch shorter, twenty pounds heavier, and much more placid than the man I had known. He told me he was out of work and had had twenty-six interviews in eight and a half months. He had gotten some out-of-town offers but had turned them down because it would cost too much to move his family.

He was unable to get the kind of job he wanted. "I've been a bridesmaid three times, but never the bride," he said. Then he told me something that made me understand why he had been disappointed in twenty-six straight interviews. He said, with conviction, "My approach is just to tell it like it is. I am what I am."

I resisted the temptation to give him advice; a shopping mall is no place to give advice on a person's interviewing style. But in other circumstances I would have said that "telling it like it is" is not so much truth telling as tension relief. His approach was an exercise in self-indulgence; he was using the interviewer as an audience for his own ego. He should have concentrated on what he could do for an employer, not on who he was as a person.

I did suggest that he weave more descriptions of his skills into his interviews. But his mind was already made up; he was not going to change. He was fatalistic about his career. He had given up in spirit, so his actions were without conviction. He had no strategy. He was just going through the motions.

Rather than making *Get Hired!* a series of prescriptions for answering specific questions, I have chosen to help you understand the skills you have to offer and use your self-appraisal to answer any questions you are asked.[1] If you spend enough time planning and practicing these techniques for answering questions, you'll be able to talk about the real you without sounding canned.

I've seen over the years how a flawed selection process often yields poor matches between the tasks that need to be done and the people hired to do them, and of how an organization can falter and its people suffer as a result. I believe that prejudice and stereotypes work to everyone's disadvantage. I've watched unqualified job seekers finesse their way into a job and excellent candidates let themselves fall victim to the prejudices of poorly trained interviewers. I've also been witness to the happy results of a careful, rational, unbiased selection process. This book translates these beliefs and experiences into the actions you need to take in order to improve your interviewing effectiveness.

NEW WAYS OF WORKING

I've also seen how the accelerating pace of change has overtaken the job market over the last few years. Change is the only thing you can be sure of now. The job you had six months ago has already changed. The job you're going to have next month will change before you get it. The dream career you planned five years ago has probably evaporated. Everything about a job that you had once, have now, or want to have is changing.[2]

The forces driving this transformation are many and complex. Technological changes and global competition are two of the most obvious. To survive in this climate, organizations must get more work done with fewer skilled workers, fewer information managers, fewer layers of management. Individual employees must adapt to constantly changing performance requirements. New kinds of work require new ways to assign tasks; self-directed work teams take the place of individual jobs.

The traditional concept of the job is becoming a relic of the past, at least in large corporations. If you're interviewing for a newly created job, chances are the organization doesn't know enough about what it needs to write a job description. Even if you stay in your current job, in three years the work you're doing will probably be different. If you're reading this book to prepare for a promotional interview, the odds are that the job you want will change as well. On the bright side, if you hate your current job, the odds are that it, too, will change. These clouds have silver linings.

NEW WAYS OF HIRING

As the concept of the job has evolved, so has the interview. More and more attention is being paid to finding not just a likeable person but a worker with a specific set of skills who can adapt as job requirements change. The result is an overall trend toward a more scientific selection process. However, there continue to be many different styles of interviewing.

Each organization may have its own style of interviewing, usually an amalgam of two or more identifiable techniques. It's hard for you to know what to expect. Will the interview be a friendly chat with a sympathetic listener, or a grilling by a gang of flinty-eyed interrogators? Will there be personal questions? Will your answers be scored, or will the interviewer use a general impression to make a decision?

As you will see, not knowing what sort of interview you will encounter doesn't have to hurt your chances. If you prepare for what appears to be the most effective kind of interview the organization can use—a behavioral-based interview—you will almost automatically present the best case for yourself. You will communicate your job-related skills honestly and effectively, and you will help the interviewer base the hiring decision primarily on your true qualifications.

In fact, preparing for the behavioral-based interview highlights your strengths in any type of selection process—new hires, promotions, internal placements. It prompts you to discover, rediscover, or examine your own strengths and weaknesses and search for the kinds of jobs you are best suited for. It helps you redefine your skills for your employer. It shows a potential new employer how you can contribute to its productivity. Not least, it gives you a positive outlook on the ordeal of looking for employment and helps you keep your dignity in any interview situation, no matter how inept, hostile, or biased the interviewer.

Not everyone finds the job search a totally negative experience. In a recent conversation, one person who had found himself out in the cold told me, "I was devastated at first. It took me completely by surprise. But I soon found that the really important things in life didn't change at all. Something as simple as taking my son to little league gave me the foundation I needed for moving on."

Another candidate was delighted to be in her job search. It was an exciting challenge. She said, "After a little bit, I discovered that most interviewers are so bad that just a little bit of preparation would make me do well. With disciplined, systematic preparation, I could hold my own with any interviewer."

YOUR PERSONAL JOB COACH

I've been through the job jungle from east to west and north to south, and I've seen it from high and low. My company, Behavioral Technology®, has conducted more than a thousand workshops on interviewing with organizations such as Hewlett-Packard, Federal Express, and the Internal Revenue Service. I know how good and how bad the interviewing process can be. To achieve success in my line of work, I've had to learn from other people's mistakes and communicate the lessons to them and to others. This book is designed to pass on the lessons to you.

Think of me as your personal job coach. Of course, I can't be like your tennis coach or your golf pro because you are here and I am somewhere else. Our interaction is limited by the fact that I must speak to you through this book. But I will use these pages to show you how to tap your own natural strengths, your experience, your personal resources, and some of the outside resources available to you that you may not be aware of. I'll coach you on how to present yourself to make the best impression on those who will decide whether to hire you.

I will encourage you to take an honest, realistic approach to getting a job. If you've interviewed before, you already know that some interviewers can be devious and misleading, encouraging you to blurt out things that can hurt your job chances. Others enjoy wielding power and having the job seeker at their mercy. A good interviewer will treat you with dignity and encourage you to make your best case. The exercises and techniques outlined in this book will help you keep your dignity in the presence of the worst interviewers and make the most of the opportunities afforded you by the rest.

DOING YOUR PART

If we were face-to-face and I were coaching you on the major and minor points of slam-dunking an interview, you would turn to me at times and say, "Yeah, but. . . ." Then I could counter with a more detailed or reasoned explanation of my point. Since I can't defend my ideas to you in person, I'll try throughout this book to anticipate your "yeah-buts" and cover as many of the bases as I can.

But much of the responsibility must necessarily fall on you—that is, you must read beyond my words, extend the principles I'm communicating, to work out some of the answers for yourself. Remember, you are the expert on the particular job search you find yourself in. Read the book, analyze the situation, and apply whatever is appropriate. If I were your golf pro, I could tell you which club is best for getting out of the rough a hundred yards from the fourth green. But if you were playing on a strange course in another town, you'd have to remember the general principles I taught you and figure it out for yourself.

Don't let one bad experience with an interviewer, or two, or five, keep you from pursuing your dream job. If they don't hire you, think of it as *their* loss. It's not your role to help an interviewer rise above his or her inadequacy. Your task is to get hired, and if you keep moving, you will. Think of me as running along beside you, telling you not to quit.

An in-person coach is also there to spur you on, to defend you from your doubts, to help you to get beyond your "yeah-buts." To some extent, I can do this by anticipating your fears—after all, you wouldn't be the first to let self-doubt hold you back. But you must be the one to push ahead when the going gets rough. Remember this: Doing something, taking almost any action, is better than doing nothing. Just visualize me saying to you, "Hey, just do it!" or "Nothing ventured, nothing gained!" or "Seize the day!" You're the job shark. Keep moving.

TAKE COURAGE

As a job seeker, you are starting out on a great journey—one that you may or may not have made before. On this journey you will face challenges both known and unknown. Knowing this, you are probably more than a little worried about what you will find.

You're right to be afraid. Fear is a valuable emotion. Kept under control, it sharpens your perceptions and makes you think more clearly. It will help you prepare to meet the challenges. And I'm here beside you, ready to make the journey with you.

As your personal job coach, my first advice to you is this: Stay calm, don't worry too much. You're off to a good start. This book is a map of what lies ahead of you. Reading it, understanding it, and using it will greatly increase your chances of getting a good job—a job that you will be well suited for, in an organization that knows and appreciates your strengths and talents.

Get Hired! will help you . . . **get hired!**

CHAPTER 2

SURF
THE
TRENDS

Dreams and opportunities differ in an important way. Dreams engage your passion for taking action. Opportunities invite you to act on your dreams in a practical way. There's no substitute for discovering interview opportunities that engage your sense of career destiny and apply your skills realistically. But can you realistically expect to find such opportunities in today's uncertain, unstable job market?

The answer is yes—statistically. There is much in current work-force trends and projections to both encourage you and guide you in your search for career opportunities. These trends are based on long-term changes in the population and the ongoing technology-driven revolution in work.

WATCHING FOR THE RIGHT WAVES

Identifying trends is like watching the surf come in. First, you notice the waves that are hitting the beach. They're pretty obvious. If you are in the water, you feel their power. Sometimes you get knocked down. Next, there are waves a few yards out, the ones that haven't quite broken yet. You see them well in advance, and you can get ready for them.

But the waves you really need to identify are the waves that surfers look for—the subtle swells far from shore, hardly visible, that you need to see early to get a powerful ride. The skilled surfer knows how to identify the good waves, the ones that will take him all the way in and not fizzle halfway to shore.

Just like waves in the surf, some trends don't relate to you or your needs. They're the ones that will fizzle out or break somewhere down the beach. But other trends relate to your job search in general and your interviews in particular. These are the trends that will help you compete in getting hired. These are the waves you need to surf.

Trend No. 1: The Changing Nature of Jobs

Not so long ago it was meaningful to think of getting a job that you could keep for a long time. Trade unions were built around doing particular jobs. Administrators were responsible for seeing that certain job tasks were completed. Managers built careers in getting other people to do their jobs. We thought in terms of career paths, of progressing through a series of jobs and educational experiences to a well-paid, prestigious, secure position high in some organization's management hierarchy.

But this concept of a job has been fading as the pace of change accelerates and more and more segments of the economy are affected.[1] New technologies burst into being, new companies vie in global market warfare, old industries die, new organizations are formed to deal with the problems of change. Fewer factory workers are needed—and in these lean, mean times, still fewer corporate managers. Service-based employment multiplies, especially in medical, security, food, and information services.

Lost in the melee are old jobs—indeed, even the old concept of the job. Consider this: In the last year of your current or most recent job, how many times did the work change? When I ask this question in a seminar, I hear chuckles and sighs. Very few have job descriptions that are current.

The work you're hired to do changes—and so must you. So when you're hired on now, you're no longer considered the human half of the employee-job unit. You're hired as an adaptable asset, the owner of an expandable set of skills

YEAH-BUT

I know I need to learn new skills, but I'm too old to go back to school!

COACH'S COMEBACK

Maybe you don't really need another degree. Many organizations train their own personnel as their needs and jobs change. What skills does your organization need? What will it need in the near future? Go straight to the nearest bookstore or library; go online; attend seminars. Keep your mind open and your skill base growing. Become your own university.

that can be applied to whatever tasks need doing, today and tomorrow and next year. Perhaps the most crucial of these skills is the ability to learn new skills quickly and adapt to changing task requirements.

Discrete jobs are being transformed by the trend toward self-directed work teams, in which team members apportion the work among themselves and over time. Individuals share tasks and split shifts to suit organizational and personal needs. Customer satisfaction becomes the primary objective, sometimes causing daily or even hourly changes in work assignments. Factor in changes in technology and the marketplace, and the odds become overwhelming that, whether you're still working for the same organization or another, you'll be doing something different a year from now.

So, instead of being involved in a job search, think of yourself as engaged in a work search. This will make a big difference in the way you approach an interview. If you can identify the work to be done in an organization and communicate the skills that you have for doing that work, then you may be able to identify work that needs to be done even when no "jobs" are available. Then you can help your potential employer create a job, and you can fine tune your answers to interview questions.

Trend No. 2: Occupational Evolution

Although it's often possible to persuade the interviewer that her organization has an unrecognized need for your skills, you should be careful not to try to sell

---

YEAH-BUT

I'm no good at learning new technologies.

COACH'S COMEBACK

It may surprise you to hear that the newer technologies are getting easier to use. Computers work more intuitively. Machines now do some things automatically that you used to find difficult to learn. For example, it's easier to set up a computer to print personalized letters for mass mailings. Invest a few hours; discover the latest technologies you need to learn. It will save you hours of hard work and years of sweating in a low-paying job.

---

the interviewer on the kind of work *you* want to do rather than adapting to what the organization needs to have done. You need to be able to list and describe your skills, of course, but stay alert to what the interviewer is asking. Even if the job in question is in your specialty, you may not be aware of how the skill requirements have changed, or how they may differ from one organization to another. If you have a reasonable level of skill in a high-growth area and are willing to learn, the odds are that you can pass most interviews for a high-growth job. If you're inflexible and not willing to learn, you're in for a lot of frustration.

You can increase your chances of finding work by paying close attention to occupational trends. Looking for jobs in stagnant or declining fields is unlikely to get you an interview, much less a career. Although there's a lot to be said for being single-minded and staying focused on your dream, trying to sell an employer on your typewriter repair skills is a lost cause. You'll have a better chance of success if you adapt your aspirations and skills to occupational trends.

The U.S. Department of Labor's projections through the year 2005 indicate some areas of expected job growth and some occupations it might be better to leave behind. For example, the number of peripheral data-processing equipment operators is expected to fall to less than half of 1992 levels—but jobs for systems analysts will more than double. The clear message: Forget about operating data-processing equipment and start looking for courses in systems analysis. Better yet, interview with an organization that will train you, and tell them you're eager to learn.

Trend No. 3: The Quest for Diversity

One trend that touches every job candidate is the diversification of the work force. The Hudson Institute's Work Force 2000 study[2] describes this phenomenon clearly. Among the study's findings are these:

- Almost two-thirds of new entrants in the U.S. work force between 1987 and 2000 will be women. By the year 2000, 61 percent of all women of working age are expected to have jobs.

- African-Americans, Hispanics, and other minorities will make up 15.5 percent of the work force in 2000, up from 11.1 percent in 1970. Altogether, nonwhites will make up about 29 percent of the new work-force entrants between 1987 and 2000.

- Nonwhites, women, and immigrants combined will constitute more than five-sixths of the net additions to the work force between 1987 and 2000.

- The number of younger workers will fall by two million, hitting smaller businesses and the food service industry especially hard.

These statistics have great significance for every job candidate. Both the *composition* of the work force and the types of jobs *available* will change greatly.

YEAH-BUT

I'm a caucasian male. Diversity doesn't relate to me.

COACH'S COMEBACK

Yes it does. You can have a competitive advantage over the caucasian males who are not sensitive to diversity issues. If you can focus your attention on job tasks and team efforts without commenting on the personal differences among people, then you can be a better fit than many. It's okay to recognize differences, but don't mention them.

FASTEST GROWING OCCUPATIONS

Projected employment growth by occupation (percentage increase), 1994–2005

Workers in over half of the twenty fastest growing occupations are involved in providing health or social services.

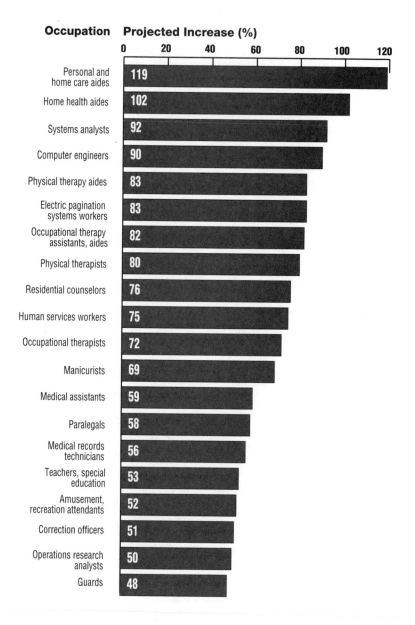

Occupation	Projected Increase (%)
Personal and home care aides	119
Home health aides	102
Systems analysts	92
Computer engineers	90
Physical therapy aides	83
Electric pagination systems workers	83
Occupational therapy assistants, aides	82
Physical therapists	80
Residential counselors	76
Human services workers	75
Occupational therapists	72
Manicurists	69
Medical assistants	59
Paralegals	58
Medical records technicians	56
Teachers, special education	53
Amusement, recreation attendants	52
Correction officers	51
Operations research analysts	50
Guards	48

Projected employment growth by occupation (in thousands), 1994–2005

Occupational growth will be very concentrated. The following twenty occupations are projected to account for more than 40 percent of total employment growth. Three of them are among the twenty fastest growing occupations.

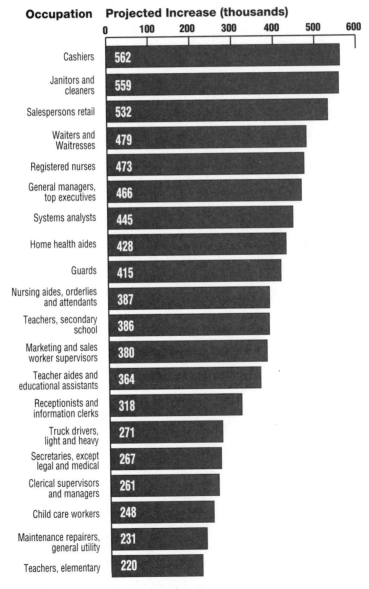

Occupation	Projected Increase (thousands)
Cashiers	562
Janitors and cleaners	559
Salespersons retail	532
Waiters and Waitresses	479
Registered nurses	473
General managers, top executives	466
Systems analysts	445
Home health aides	428
Guards	415
Nursing aides, orderlies and attendants	387
Teachers, secondary school	386
Marketing and sales worker supervisors	380
Teacher aides and educational assistants	364
Receptionists and information clerks	318
Truck drivers, light and heavy	271
Secretaries, except legal and medical	267
Clerical supervisors and managers	261
Child care workers	248
Maintenance repairers, general utility	231
Teachers, elementary	220

Source: "The American Work Force: 1994–2005."[3]

At first, the main goal many companies pursued in developing a diverse work force was to avoid being charged with discriminatory hiring practices. Now, however, demographic changes give a clear economic advantage to a company whose work force mirrors the nation's ethnic diversity. Why is this so?

- Customers appreciate organizations whose workers are like them.

- International business relationships demand enlightened attitudes toward individual differences.

- A racist or sexist work environment causes top candidates to go to competitors.

- An organization that doesn't recruit older workers will have difficulty staffing entry-level jobs.

The demand for diversity translates into opportunities for everyone. It signifies a shift in organizational thinking. Organizations seek to build a work force with noticeable differences for reasons of economy, flexibility, competition, customer service, and productivity. Because of this, the things about you as a person that might once have denied you opportunities now make you more attractive to many employers.

Trend No. 4: The Changing Infrastructure of Work

To operate effectively, organizations need an infrastructure of resources around them—such things as government services, vendors, natural resources, and a work force. Because of this need, organizations create jobs not only within themselves but all around them as well. Each of the channels into the organization has work opportunities you can explore.

YEAH-BUT

There are no large companies in my town.

COACH'S COMEBACK

Most of the jobs being created these days are in small or start-up companies. Find one near you that is growing, and get in on the ground floor—or join another small business that will provide services for it.

Our company, Behavioral Technology®, has acquired major industry and government clients by virtue of being near the headquarters of Federal Express. This high-performance company has grown an infrastructure of work and made Memphis a major national distribution center. Government has benefited, banks have benefited, the University of Memphis has benefited, real estate developers have benefited, consulting firms have benefited. I, too, have benefited. I had the privilege of presenting its first management training in 1975 and conducting interviews for Federal Express in the '70s and '80s.

Just south of my home in Memphis is the town of Tunica, Mississippi. In the last three years the area around Tunica has acquired several casinos and become a "Little Las Vegas." Towns and counties have had to improve their government services—fire departments, police, schools, roads. Businesses providing services and products to the casinos have expanded and multiplied. Now it's hard to get skilled construction, restaurant, and hotel workers in Memphis; the high-paying jobs in Tunica, Mississippi, have opened up employment opportunities and raised salaries all the way back into Tennessee.

When my brother moved to Huntsville, Alabama, in the mid '60s, he had the only house in a new subdivision on the outskirts of town. Huge sums were being spent in the space industry, especially on start-up research and vendor development projects in Huntsville. Within five years his suburb was bustling with restaurants, churches, gas stations, and other thriving businesses.

Wherever government or any large organization invests heavily, you will likely find an infrastructure of work that can create opportunities for you. Study the U.S. Chamber of Commerce's listing of high-growth cities. If you're a physician, set up your first practice in a high-growth city. If you're a banker, go where the need for money will grow fast. If you're a cabinetmaker, go where the new homes are being built. For any career, you can find plenty of opportunity if you're willing to follow the money and go where the infrastructure is.

Trend No. 5: The Conceptual Superstructure of Work

Just as technology is changing the work infrastructure, management science is revolutionizing the superstructure, raising organizational performance with new strategies for improving work effectiveness.

YEAH-BUT

I'm trained as a supervisor; I don't know how to do anything else.

COACH'S COMEBACK

Because computers have taken over much of the work of information management, supervisors are becoming an endangered species. Hierarchy is out, work teams are in. Learn to work collegially in project teams. Enhance your communication skills. Adapt.

Much of the recent change in work improvement can be traced to W. Edwards Deming. Dr. Deming's approach to performance improvement emphasizes the use of work teams to constantly improve performance. His name is associated with the quality movement, continuous improvement, and effective work systems—strategies that Japanese manufacturers used to challenge American industry.

Many other books have advocated the restructuring of work to meet customer needs, improve work systems, and speed the delivery of value. *In Search of Excellence*, by Tom Peters and Robert Waterman, grabbed the attention of managers with its practical emphasis on quality, value, and the customer.[4] Peters' subsequent *Thriving on Chaos*[5] and *The Pursuit of Wow!*[6] further describe the importance of serving the customer through innovation and commitment.

Reengineering the Organization, by Hammer and Champy, emphasizes the roles of individuals and teams in improving performance.[7] However, rather than continuous improvement, they recommend revolutionary changes in the structure of work. There is emphasis on the roles of internal and external customers and the involvement of work teams in the change process.

Changes in the conceptual superstructure of work in the government are reflected in *Reinventing Government*, Vice President Al Gore's treatise on how government can be made to work better and cost less.[8] The National Performance Review that Gore initiated was aimed at bringing about four kinds of change:

- Cutting red tape
- Putting customers first
- Empowering employees to get results
- Cutting back to basics

This study has led to recommendations that parallel the changes taking place in business.

The changing superstructure of work creates new employment opportunities of a special kind. If you like to work with little supervision, to assume responsibility for your own work and the work of your team, then you should seek out this new type of organization. Here's how to identify them. Look for organizations that

- design work around customer needs
- use work teams that need little supervision
- are "reinventing" themselves
- measure their level of service to customers
- have high levels of change-for-improvement

Today's "new" organization is not everyone's cup of tea. Many find it too difficult to set their own goals, share team responsibility, and exercise their initiative to adapt quickly to shifting conditions. Be honest with yourself. Would you rather work under direct supervision with unchanging, clearly defined duties and lines of responsibility? Are you just looking for a job? If so, you're better off looking for routine work in an organization with a conventional structure—one that is clearly managed from the top down, with little emphasis on teams, improvement, or the customer.

Trend No. 6: More Specific Selection Criteria

Like tax returns and fitness plans, jobs these days come with tasks and instructions that are a lot more detailed than they used to be. The tasks may change frequently, but they are usually well defined for the moment. For basic jobs, human resources can usually provide you a listing of the education, technical knowledge, and skills required. Higher-level jobs, which usually involve more technical or management skills, specify competencies such as conflict management, team building, and adaptability.

Employers have become more specific about their selection objectives for two reasons. First, organizational change puts a new emphasis on job design

YEAH-BUT

What if I don't have the exact skills they need?

COACH'S COMEBACK

Chances are, neither does much of your competition. Present the skills you have as thoroughly and impressively as you can. The employers will choose the best combination they can find, and may consider many factors they haven't specified. Communicate the benefits of your particular package of assets.

and quality of work. More thought is given to how each task contributes to an organizational objective, and to the skills and qualities needed to perform that task. Second, a hiring process that is not specific about the selection criteria and the qualifications necessary for doing the job well is suspected of being overly subjective—that is, discriminatory—and invites legal problems.

Many organizations now base their selection criteria on "core competencies"—written descriptions of the performance factors deemed important in a variety of management and nonmanagement positions. These competencies are often directly linked to the organization's mission statement and reflect the values in the organization's culture. Because core competencies are designed to help individual contributors and teams perform, they are widely disseminated throughout the organization. In many cases, they are public information, available to job candidates.

Competency statements reflect the growing desire of organizations to be job related and specific in the way they conduct selection interviews. The organization treats each competency statement as a selection criterion and designs questions around it. If the job you are being considered for requires leadership, you might expect to be asked questions that directly relate to that competency.

Many organizations use competencies to develop lists of questions for job-specific structured interviews. The interviewer comes prepared with questions about specific skills that are important for doing a particular job. Instead of being asked about your general integrity, you might find yourself responding to questions about something as specific as ethical decisions you made in dealing with a printing vendor in your last job.

USE THE TRENDS TO YOUR ADVANTAGE

Trend	Action
Jobs Are Dying	Conduct a work search, not a job search
	Give specifics on your team skills
Occupational Evolution	Learn new technical skills
	Interview for growth jobs
The Quest for Diversity	Explain how you contribute to diversity
	Explain how you can work with all people
The Changing Infrastructure of Work	Identify high-growth regions for interviews
	Target the vendors to major employers
The Conceptual Superstructure of Work	Talk about flexibility and teamwork
	Give specifics on several skills you offer
More Specific Selection Criteria	Learn new technical skills
	Give specifics on the exact skills you offer

As you prepare for an interview, keep in mind the trend toward basing hiring decisions on specialized qualifications. To help the recruiter decide which position you should interview for, you must be able to say exactly what you do well. For example:

- "I know twenty-seven software packages well enough to instruct end users."
- "I regularly worked fifty hours a week in my last job."
- "I can write a newsletter with no grammatical mistakes."
- "I'm good at developing new business by cold calling."

You may discover as well that you set yourself apart from other candidates by simply describing how your specific skills will benefit the employer.

BEYOND JOB MARKET TRENDS

Now you know more about the job market you face as you get ready to make the transition into a new work situation. How can you use this knowledge to *ace the interview?* It depends on the kind of interview, as you'll see in the next chapter.

CHAPTER 3

THE FOUR
INTERVIEW STYLES

An interview is a little like a baseball game. You're the batter, the interviewer is the pitcher. Each pitcher is different; each has a repertoire of pitches that he can deliver, depending on his inclinations and the game situation. You need to be able to hit whatever he throws at you—fast balls, sliders, change-ups, screwballs—even the occasional slow, easy pitch. When you're standing at the plate, bat in hand, you can't know for sure what the next pitch will be. You must be ready to hit all kinds of pitches from all kinds of pitchers. You need to anticipate, prepare, and practice to get to first base.

But in crucial ways an interview is easier. Unlike a baseball game, an interview is a contest that both you and the interviewer can win. You can respond in a way that uses each question to your best advantage, while still satisfying the needs of the interviewer. It's as though you could grab hold of an incoming pitch and bring it over the plate at exactly the right spot, hit it safely for a double—and make the pitcher like it. Once you can read the interviewer's style and anticipate what kinds of questions he will throw at you, you will know how to respond in a way that meets his needs. In the interview game, your real competition is all the other batters, not the pitcher.

This chapter, by exploring the most common interview styles, will help you anticipate what the interviewer will say and do. Your assessment of the interviewer's style will help you manage your self-presentation and phrase your answers accordingly. Keep in mind, however, that most interviewers are not pure examples of any one type. Every interviewer uses a different combination of gut-feel, personality assessment, value clarification, and structure; but there is a way you can prepare for the unknown, and it's not as hard as you may think.

THE DIMENSIONS OF INTERVIEW STYLE

Here's an easy way to understand the different types of interviews you can encounter. Visualize two scales, crossed at right angles. Each represents one aspect of interview style. The horizontal scale shows what kinds of information the interviewer tries to get from you; it ranges from person oriented at the left end to job oriented on the right. The vertical scale, which shows how the interviewer gathers and manages information, ranges from intuitive to structured.

In a person-oriented interview, the interviewer tries to discover your personal characteristics—the impressions you generate, your personality traits, and your feelings. A job-oriented interviewer, on the other hand, wants to know about your work experience, your skills, and your work-related values in order to determine how well you might perform the tasks needed to get the job done. The job-related strategy is the approach industrial psychologists and attorneys typically recommend because, to be valid, the interview must be job related.

The vertical scale shows how the interviewer asks questions. An intuitive interviewer has no particular plan or agenda but asks questions spontaneously, as they come to mind, based on the interviewer's experience and impressions of the candidate. This type of interviewer usually takes few notes. A typical structured interviewer, by contrast, asks every candidate the same standard set of questions (usually written out in advance), asks follow-up probes that relate only to the question, and takes extensive notes in order to recall and later evaluate your answers.

The structured approach may feel more regimented, even rigid. But it is intrinsically fairer because it requires the interviewer to be more objective. The

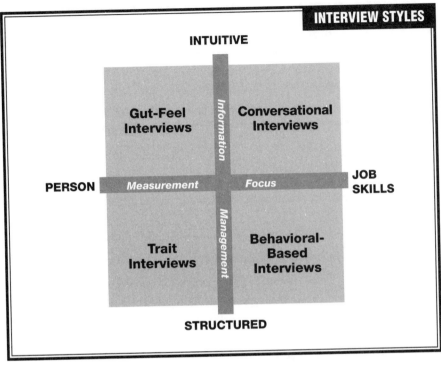

intuitive interview feels more open and relaxed; the interviewer asks questions as they occur to him, based on his feelings, perceptions, and intuitions about you and your skills. This approach may feel more comfortable, but it allows for subjective interpretation of your answers. It may also lead to legal problems if the interviewer carelessly asks a question about a legally protected topic.

A simple way to categorize the four interview styles that you will encounter is to relate them to the two crossed scales:

- Gut-feel interviews are intuitive and person related.
- Trait interviews are structured and person related.
- Conversational interviews are intuitive and job related.
- Behavioral-based interviews are structured and job related.

As soon as the interview begins, you will begin to pick up clues as to which of these four categories your interview falls into. Does the interviewer use a structured interview form? Are follow-up probes related to the job? Is she more interested in you as a person, or in your job experience and skills?

Regardless of which style the interviewer uses—and most use a combination of styles rather than a pure form—you will usually come out ahead if you respond by giving specific examples of things you have done that will provide

---

COACH'S TIP

Instead of trying to analyze the interviewer's style during the interview, adopt a general strategy that will fit most styles. In answering most interview questions, give specific examples of "times when" you used a skill at work. This will enable you to prepare honest, accurate information about what you have to offer to the job. Then, if you can assess the interviewer's style quickly, you can modify this general strategy during the interview.

---

evidence of your skills. This approach will satisfy the behavioral-based interviewer; it will give the conversational interviewer the information needed to make a good decision; it will document your characteristics for a trait interviewer; and it will help you persuade the gut-feel interviewer that you will be a good fit for the job.

GUT-FEEL INTERVIEWS

The gut-feel interview uses a person-related, intuitive approach to see how you measure up to subjective selection criteria. In this type of interview, general impressions are a valid basis for selecting or rejecting you. There is no systematic attempt to gather information about your skills for doing the job. The gut-feel interviewer relies on intuition and subjective criteria to guide the interview and interpret answers. The problem for you is that it's hard—perhaps impossible—to figure out what these criteria are, or how the interviewer will assess whether you have the "right stuff." It's almost like a throw of the dice or a spin of the roulette wheel.

A surprising number of interviewers-in-training come into my classes believing they don't need to structure their interviews. Quite a few practicing interviewers share this belief. Studies have revealed that many interviewers feel they can suitably assess the candidate's skills for the job within the first few minutes of the interview.[1] This means that you will need to develop a positive first impression and keep it going during the entire interview. You cannot afford to relax your self-discipline and say the wrong thing, because this interviewer is prone to overreact to negative information. You can lose your positive momentum very quickly.

COACH'S TIP

SIGNS OF A GUT-FEEL INTERVIEW

- No structured interview form
- Questions on pet theories and illegal topics
- Little or no reference to job requirements
- Emphasis on personal characteristics
- Evaluation based on how much you are liked
- Decision based on subjective reactions

Gut-feel interviewers often base their decisions on pet theories. Many of these would seem hilarious to you—until you ran across one that denied you a job. A highly respected police commander once explained to me the most important factor in selecting police recruits: "Doc, I know it when I see it—he's tall." This pet theory, which is biased against women and some minorities, failed to account for such critical factors as skill and coping, courage, adaptability, willingness to follow procedures, and decision-making ability.

Some pet theories are marginally valid, such as the importance of grooming, education, arriving on time, and communicating well. Others are downright offensive and prejudicial: the belief that women can't handle stress or that some races are smarter than others.

PET THEORIES AND INTERVIEW QUESTIONS

Pet Theory	Question
Overweight people are lazy.	"Do you plan to go on a diet?"
Playing contact sports builds competitiveness.	"What sports have you played?"
Women with children aren't career minded.	"How are you going to take care of your kids and hold a full-time job?"
Religious people can't adapt to others.	"We're mostly liberal thinkers here. Do you think you might have trouble fitting in?"
Engineers are rigid.	"Don't you think you might have trouble adapting to new work rules?"

YEAH-BUT

I make a good first impression. Why should I worry about not doing well with a gut-feel interviewer?

COACH'S COMEBACK

Remember that interviewers' tastes differ. Your positive first impression for one gut-feel interviewer may be a big turnoff for another. Also, don't forget that there are other interview styles you may need to deal with. The best thing to do is to make a good first impression and give specific examples of how you've used your skills at work.

TRAIT INTERVIEWS

A trait interview uses an approach that is person related but structured, the goal being measurement of key personality traits such as aggression, ego strength, discipline, and friendliness. In a pure trait interview, the interviewer reads questions off a structured interview form. These questions relate more to your personal characteristics than to your job skills, often without reference to the kind of work to be done.

With a controlled, scientific approach, sometimes enhanced by personality testing, a trait assessment can be effective in assessing crucial personality traits needed for a job. But a good trait interviewer needs more training than a

---

YEAH-BUT

I've been told that I have a good personality. Why should I worry about a trait interviewer?

COACH'S COMEBACK

Many trait interviewers are prone to make snap judgments about you as a person. This means that you must be absolutely clear about what you are like. Give specific examples of things that you have done that really show why you would be good for the job.

**QUESTIONS THAT TELL YOU IT'S
A TRAIT-BASED INTERVIEW**

- To what extent are you an organized person?
- How do you evaluate yourself in terms of adaptability?
- List your most positive qualities for me.
- Are you more aggressive or relaxed in problem solving?

manager typically gets. It's easy for an untrained trait interviewer to use individual traits to stereotype a candidate, the way a gut-feel interviewer does.

Preparing for a trait interview is straightforward. Identify the traits that correspond to the things you do well—for example, perseverance, ingenuity, cooperativeness. Have these words ready to use when describing yourself. Also develop a short list of your negative traits that you can use to respond to negative probes, but try to state these negatives in as positive a light as possible. For example, one of your positive traits might be that you "like work that is challenging." Be ready to admit to your negative trait: you are "too critical of people who do not put forth strong effort." Then follow up with a specific example of a time when you took on and accomplished a challenging task.

CONVERSATIONAL INTERVIEWS

The conversational interview is an unstructured interview focusing mainly on job experience and job skills. This kind of interview resembles a conversation between two equals. There's no prepared list of questions. Instead, questions seem to arise naturally out of the flow of the conversation, based on your responses and the interviewer's knowledge of the job. The conversation often branches naturally from one topic to another, as though the interviewer had no other purpose than to get to know you better.

This impression is misleading. The conversational interviewer uses rapport, rather than structure, as the principal tool for gathering information. You may spend much of the interview in a friendly conversation about your general interests and experiences. Eventually, however, the interviewer will ask questions about your work experience. If you get into areas that are harder to discuss or that make you uncomfortable, he will steer the conversation back to

---

YEAH-BUT

I want the interviewer to know what my values are. They will work to my benefit.

COACH'S COMEBACK

Good! The best way to communicate what your values are is to show how they have guided your behavior. Ensure that your values are not seen as being "hot air" by explaining what your values caused you to do in a specific situation. Notice that this approach will also pay off with the other types of interviewers.

---

areas where you feel more relaxed. By building and maintaining rapport, the conversational interviewer hopes to make you comfortable enough to reveal important details about your qualifications and your character that you might otherwise be reluctant to mention.

In particular, the conversational interviewer is interested in your values—principles such as integrity, collegiality, and recognition that you hold important as part of your work life. Often the interviewer looks for some reflection of values that are part of a mission statement that identifies core competencies desired in all who work in the organization.

If the interview is going well, you may feel as though you're just having a friendly chat. This is a big mistake. You're being scrutinized all the time—in the interview, at the coffee station, in the car, at lunch. You may feel comfortable,

---

COACH'S TIP

HOW TO HANDLE THE CONVERSATIONAL INTERVIEW

- Build rapport with the interviewer.
- Be informal but professional.
- Show concern and care for people.
- Give examples of teamwork.
- Share your values.

but remember—this interviewer uses the friendly approach to get as much information as possible.

Many conversational interviewers are highly skilled and very knowledgeable about the job for which you are being considered. But many others fall short of the mark; without the guidance of a structured interview form, their conversations can become rambling, disjointed, ineffective sessions that produce little useful information.

BEHAVIORAL-BASED INTERVIEWS

A behavioral-based interview is structured, like the trait interview, and job focused, like the conversational approach. But it is much more than a combination of these two types. I believe that it is the most objective, systematic, consistent, and unbiased method available for filling jobs with the best people. And it is as far from a slap-dash, gut-feel interview as you can get. It is usually part of a selection system in which everyone uses the same technique—each interviewer, the group manager, the human resources representative, the campus interviewers, and senior management.[2]

The behavioral-based interview will be our point of reference through most of this book. My experience with organizations whose selection processes

---

COACH'S TIP

**QUESTIONS THAT TELL YOU IT'S
A BEHAVIORAL-BASED INTERVIEW**

- Tell me about a time when you managed conflict successfully.
- Describe a situation in which you were able to effectively tell your boss some very bad news.
- Showcase your skills in teamwork by describing a team problem that you were able to resolve.
- Describe a mistake you made in the last six months, tell me what you learned from it, and then give me an example of how you used your learning.
- When did you use common sense to justify breaking an important rule at work?

fall short of being adequate has taught me an important fact: The best way for a job candidate to approach any interview is to use the best principles and ideals of the behavioral-based approach. When a less-than-fair or marginally competent interviewer poses the kinds of questions that can't possibly get at the truth of your qualifications, respond as though you were answering a proper question in a behavioral-based interview.

In addition to the standard kind of behavioral-based interview, there are two other related types: the simulation interview and the situational interview. These three techniques can be distinguished in terms of their time frames. Standard behavioral-based interviewing deals with past behavior; a simulation interview assesses behavior in the present; a situational interview deals with future behavior. All are structured, and all deal with job skills.[3]

The Simulation Interview

In the simulation interview, you are asked to demonstrate specific abilities by performing tasks. For example, the interviewer may say,

"Here's a paper clip. Sell it to me."

As you try to sell the paper clip to the interviewer, she may play the part of an unwilling customer, expressing doubts and objections, forcing you to deal with her sales resistance. Later, in her assessment, she may note how many benefit statements you were able to come up with, how well you distinguished between features and benefits, and how skillful you were in closing.

Preparing for the simulation interview is as basic as training yourself to do the job. This type of interview has the benefit of being directly related to important job tasks; you qualify for the job by showing that you can perform the tasks.

The Situational Interview

The situational interviewer asks you hypothetical questions, each presenting a dilemma for you to solve. For example:

"You're the manager of a shipping dock in Chicago. You're at the end of a difficult quarter. The shipping manager in Atlanta calls with an emergency. He asks you to help out by lending him a driver and a truck. If you do, you'll probably fall short of your goal and miss out on your quarterly bonus—but you'll be working as a team player, which is what your boss wants you to do. What would you do in this situation?"

Each of your answers is scored on its own rating scale; your total score is used in assessing your overall performance in the interview. The best way to prepare for situational questions is to think through the difficult situations you have experienced, identify what you've learned from them, and use this information to anticipate how you would answer questions. You should also make it a point to thoroughly understand the job and the organization. This will give you the strongest clues on how to present your answers.

Behavioral-based interviewing is designed to acquire information about a person's past actions that can be used to predict how well the person will function on the job. This idea uses common sense and is academically supportable. Once we become adults, we tend to resist change. We develop habits, both good and bad, that are hard to break without concentrated effort. We also lose some awareness of these habits, so that when asked to describe how we behaved in a past situation, we tend to give a reasonably accurate picture of what we did. We may not even be aware that certain of these actions do not reflect well on us.

Key Elements of Behavioral-Based Interviewing

There are several components of the behavioral-based approach that you can use to identify the technique and prepare your responses.

Specifics communicate best. In a behavioral-based interview, you are asked singular, open-ended questions about past events. This approach encourages you to talk at length about a particular past action. For example, if the interviewer wants information about how well you get along with customers, she might ask,

"Tell me about a time when you were able to make an angry customer happy."

The phrase "a time when" prompts you to remember a specific instance of your past behavior. You are not encouraged to give general answers, such as "I always got along well with customers." When you generalize, you don't give the interviewer the specifics needed to assess your skills. The behavioral-based interview is designed to get behind the generalities and examine specific actions.

YEAH-BUT

It takes a lot of work to develop honest, specific examples that relate to my skills. Besides, I may need to fudge a little because I don't have all the skills that the interviewer would like me to have.

COACH'S COMEBACK

You may be able to fool an interviewer well enough to get a job, but you won't be able to fool your boss well enough to keep it. In the next part you will learn how to assess your skills. By giving detailed attention to developing specific examples of times when you used your skills, you will discover that you have more skills than you previously realized. That way you can be both well prepared and honest.

Structured interviews improve accuracy. The use of prepared questions ensures that all facets of your qualifications for the job are explored, and that you are given the same opportunity to make your case as every other candidate. The interviewer may read the questions in a set order or may change the order or branch off to address questions raised by your responses.

The structured interviewer usually takes notes on your answers. You should not let this intimidate you. It's in your best interest for the interviewer, who may conduct six interviews in six hours, to remember exactly what you said. Note-taking is not evaluation; that comes later.

Several interviewers expand understanding. If you're being considered for a nonmanagement, individual-contributor job, you may be interviewed by just one person, the one who makes the hiring decision. Most organizations, however, assign more than one interviewer to assess your skills. You might have a series of separate one-hour interviews, with each interviewer asking you different questions and meeting later to discuss your answers.

On the other hand, you may get to meet all your interviewers at once. In a team interview, sometimes called a panel interview, several interviewers ask questions in rotation about your technical knowledge and work habits. This type of interview can work to your advantage: if you're well prepared, you can respond with confidence, while your competition may feel intimidated by the group setting.

Contrary examples ensure representative responses. One distinctive feature of a behavioral-based interview is the request for contrary information. No one's work life is an unbroken string of triumphs; we all learn from our mistakes and missteps. To get a better picture of your capabilities and your capacity for learning from experience, the behavioral-based interviewer may follow up a positive question with a negative. For example, "Give me an example of a time when you settled a dispute between members of your team" might be followed by "Now tell me about an instance when you weren't able to keep a disagreement from getting out of hand."

Most of us naturally want to present ourselves in the best possible light. Unless specifically asked, we aren't likely to talk about our shortcomings. But there's a big advantage to discussing your failures—it lets you describe for the interviewer how you've learned from your mistakes and overcome them. In doing so, you're demonstrating that when you next fall short of perfection, as everyone inevitably does, you will learn from it and improve your performance.

LOOKING AHEAD

Now that you know more about the job market and what you can expect in the interview, you're ready to start the self-assessment that will prepare you to ace the interview. In the next part, you'll prepare yourself emotionally for the task of selling yourself. You'll learn to identify and catalog your skills, to connect them with the benefits your potential employer might derive from them, and to frame your answers to interview questions in a succinct form that helps the interviewer recognize your strengths. Not least, you will learn ways to anticipate and overcome those dreaded "killer" questions that you'd rather not have to answer.

Remember, you're not alone. More and more people are looking for jobs today, even those who used to think theirs were safe. Having read this far, you're already better prepared to meet the challenge. You've pulled a little ahead of the field. The rest of this book will give you a true competitive advantage.

PART TWO

TAKE STOCK OF YOURSELF

As one engineer put it, "It's cold, dark, and lonely out there. I used to think of a job search as a way to better myself. Now it's a matter of career survival. If my skills are not an exact match for the job I want, chances are someone else out there will get it.

"I've been writing programs for fifteen years, but I missed out on that training job because I've used only eight current business packages. The person who got the job had only three years of work experience but was skilled with twenty-three business packages. I'm confident that I have more general computer skills, but the person who had the specialized skills got the job.

"I'm shocked at how fast things are changing. The competition for good jobs is everywhere, and the candidates are strong and highly motivated. The scary thing is that if I really knew how qualified the competition was, I might stop trying. I'd work toward my fantasy career—open that ostrich ranch I've been dreaming about for years."

This brief story touches on everything I'm going to tell you in the next five chapters.

The engineer feels alone and fearful, shocked by the competition, ready to bail out and become a rancher. That's the way many people feel, fighting the employment wars—so although he feels lonely, he's not alone. He has a tough battle ahead with his emotions, mainly to keep his lack of confidence from becoming self-perpetuating. He's scared that he "might stop trying."

The engineer feels at a great competitive disadvantage to candidates who have more software experience. Actually, the number of software programs he can run might well be less important than persuading his potential employers that the skills he has will work to their benefit and that he is willing and eager to learn others as needed, since their skill requirements will surely change over time. He can increase his chances by framing his responses to interview questions in an honest way that will help the interviewer conclude that he has the basic qualifications for the job, is adaptable, and is motivated to add to and improve his skills.

This part of the book addresses these issues. Chapter 4 will tell you ways to recognize and harness the riot of emotions that you are probably experiencing as you try to come to grips with this great change in your life—looking for new work. Chapter 5 will help you identify in writing the first impressions, traits, values, and skills that define you; chapter 6 will show you how to explain the benefits that these characteristics offer a prospective employer. And chapters 7 and 8 will afford you practice in framing persuasive answers to the interviewer's questions—even the killers.

CHAPTER 4

GET YOUR
HEAD ON
STRAIGHT

We all know someone who's an emotional disaster—someone who overreacts to criticism, worries about things that can't be controlled, and fears rejection. Watching this person deal with a problem is watching a wreck about to happen. You want to say, "Get a grip on yourself! Chill out! Relax! Things will be okay!" but you know it won't do any good, so you don't.

And we all know someone at the other end of the scale—cold, detached, and aloof. This person doesn't seem to care about life or people. Emotionally oblivious to real problems, he doesn't react to things that are disasters for others; he lets things take care of themselves. He seems so removed, so distant, that you want to say, "Hello, anybody home?" But, of course, you don't.

Who are these people? They are us—you and me—at times. You're probably like neither of these extremes—most of the time, at least—but sometimes you're fearful, nervous, excitable, and sometimes you're just too bummed out to get worked up about anything.

Now I want to remind you of something you probably already know: the interview is a place of great opportunities and pitfalls. In the interview, some emotional states can help you and some can hurt you—and they aren't necessarily the ones you might think. The "negative" emotions of pain and fear often get in the way of action and confidence, but they can work to your advantage if you transform their energy into a determination to succeed, despite your doubts. And the "positive" emotions of joy and confidence, although an important source of great energy and creativity, can work against you if you let them make you seem complacent, arrogant, or flaky.

It takes a level head to master your feelings without going to the other extreme and seeming complacent. The time you're most likely to come across as either too emotional or too cold is in a tense situation—especially an interview. This is the time when you have to say to yourself, "Chill out," or "Loosen up." In the interview, you should try to level off your feelings: stay in control, but stay open.

LET THE FEELINGS FLOW

As you prepare for your interview, you will naturally experience a wide range of emotions, from "I'm in!" to "Aw, what's the use?" You'll sweat about your college transcript, grind your teeth over your last employer, turn cartwheels because you figure you've got the next job sewed up, and go cold thinking about the unemployment line. Two hours later you'll be entertaining fantasies about sailing to Tahiti and living in a grass shack, painting masterpieces, and living on fish and pineapple with your soul mate.

These ups and downs are a normal response to the stress of anticipating the interview. They're like stage fright, an emotion that is rarely fatal but usually helpful in getting ready for a performance. Let the feelings flow now; don't worry about worrying. By the time you've finished preparing for the interview, as you will have done if you follow my advice in subsequent chapters, your nerves will be steadier and you'll appear self-possessed to the interviewer, even if underneath your veneer the butterflies are raging.

Your best strategy is to let your emotions ebb and flow while you're preparing for the interview—that is, when you're alone and there's nobody around to be injured by the shrapnel. But keep them under control when you're one-on-one with the interviewer. In the same way that you must keep your emotions from ruling your work life, you must keep them from taking over the interview. Giving focused answers means responding appropriately to the interviewer's questions, not communicating how you feel at the moment.

This does not mean that you should act like a robot, of course. The interviewer expects normal emotional responses. If you're stiff and unresponsive, you'll seem cold, distant, perhaps arrogant. Some of the interviewer's questions will arouse memories of triumphs and failures, good friends and enemies. If you're relaxed, if you've worked out your feelings beforehand, you can respond with appropriate feelings—humor, pensiveness, forthrightness—to these questions.

PROFIT FROM NEGATIVE FEELINGS

Nobody likes to feel fear, anxiety, or distress. We put a lot of effort and attention into avoiding these feelings in everyday life. Yet they are inevitable, especially when we're put into new, unfamiliar, or dangerous situations. Major life changes are accompanied by just such uncertainties, and a job search is surely a sign of a major life change.

AN EMOTIONAL AUDIT

Each of the following emotions is presented in terms of opposites. Check the left-side or the right-side emotion that is most characteristic of how you feel about your interviews. Then circle the emotions that you want to restrain during your interviews.

Negative Emotions	Positive Emotions
Anxiety over interview pressure	High confidence about interviewing
Anger about being terminated	Joy over leaving the old job
Concern over my skills/education	Belief in my skills/education
Worry over my references	Confidence in my references
Fear of losing career momentum	Accepting different opportunities
Concern over moving	Excitement over moving
Anger over politics at work	Political understanding
Disappointment with myself	Pride of personal behavior and integrity
Dislike of change	Excitement about a new job
Fear of being rejected	Acceptance of rejection

YEAH-BUT

I've always been told just to be myself. Are you telling me to hide my feelings?

COACH'S COMEBACK

No. I'm telling you to control the expression of your emotions. This does not mean being dishonest—just practical. The way you feel, good or bad, about your work search can distract the interviewer from fully exploring your job skills. By controlling the feelings you express, you help focus the interviewer's attention on what you can actually do on the job.

You may have noticed how tired such negative emotions can make you feel. That's because they use up a lot of your energy. Fear, in particular, increases your production of adrenalin, raising your metabolism. It's a survival adaptation; your body is getting ready to fight or run from a threat.

The problem is, most of the things that arouse fear in civilized people these days are not things that can be dealt with physically. So the fear goes on and on, waiting for something to happen that you can react to. That's what anxiety is, and it can rob you of the will to act on your own behalf. And all that energy goes to waste—unless you set your mind the task of harnessing it and making it work to your advantage.

Pain

A job search can involve a lot of pain. I've heard stories ranging from wounded dignity to financial ruin and broken families. But one of the most distressing things I have seen is the low-level, long-lasting pain that seems to hang like a small black cloud above people who have lost hope of finding good work. Whoever you are, whatever your skills, wherever you live, it can happen to you.

What can turn a proud, skilled, motivated employee into a downtrodden chronic job seeker? A multitude of things, both personal and impersonal. The impersonal include economic trends that have gripped individuals like a permanent drought: downsizing, competition, technological change, world markets. Personal slings and arrows include every form of legal and illegal discrimination imaginable, promises made but not kept by people you trusted, and the humiliation of being laid off, with its implication that you are not as good as the others.

Often the frustration gets worse when common-sense solutions don't seem to work. You target fine-tuned résumés and cover letters to hundreds of employers and are offered only two or three interviews. Your support group eventually gets stale and repetitive. Advice from your spouse, parents, or friends, however well meaning and loving, becomes trite after a few months. Your telephone becomes a recurring fixture in your nightmares. You'd love to hear about a job, but you hate to call new people to ask for an interview.

But if you can turn it around, you can make your pain work for you. When you channel it into a strategy, it can give you strength and conviction. Some derive strength from sharing experiences with a supportive friend or group. Others benefit from career counseling or from reading inspirational material. Still others treat pain as a challenge; they ask themselves hard questions, then answer them. Whatever works, do it. The energy you create by channeling your pain becomes positive energy for your interviews.

Here are the positive effects of channeling pain into productive energy:
- Intense feelings can help you construct a vision of your dream job.
- Psychological pain can motivate you to look for interview leads.
- Negative emotions can lead to healthy exercise.
- Bad feelings expand awareness of what you need to fix in your career.

Fear

Fear is a feeling of apprehension about something specific. You may fear things that have not happened but could, such as spilling your coffee or being beaten out by your competition. On the other hand, the source of your fear may be something that is very real, such as knowing that the interviewer is someone who actively discriminates against people like you. You can identify what you fear, and other people might agree that your fear has a reasonable basis.

Fear can be a very productive emotion. A reasonable fear of hazards keeps you alive and healthy. Even in the absence of physical danger, it can focus your attention on preparing well for an interview. It can motivate you to find out more about the skills needed for the job, to formulate answers to difficult questions you may be asked, to plan how you will speak to avoid sounding stupid.

Anxiety is different, and harder to deal with. It is a diffuse fear—a generalized worry or apprehension about nothing in particular, or about something you can't quite put your finger on. Anxiety can range from a vague uneasiness to an intense and debilitating dread. Some people become so anxious that they need to be hospitalized.

If you have interview anxiety, you have all the symptoms of fear without any immediately obvious cause. You may feel anxious around authority figures because you had a bad sergeant in the army. You may be anxious about completing a written aptitude test because you once blew a crucial college exam. Sometimes, with introspection, you can identify the source of such anxieties and neutralize them. In severe cases, a counselor can help you resolve them.

Many great people in history have learned to convert their fears and anxieties to courage, to channel into a powerful self-confidence the emotions that were otherwise a barrier to action—to change weakness to strength. Winston Churchill overcame debilitating depression and early career disasters; Franklin Delano Roosevelt triumphed over paralysis; Helen Keller conquered blindness and deafness to gain worldwide admiration. You can be certain that among the difficulties they had to surmount were fears and anxieties about their condition and their future.

You can convert fear into courage using a technique psychologists call "flooding." It is based on the idea that by trying to make yourself feel fearful you can actually inhibit your fear. Although used primarily to deal with phobias and deep-seated problems, flooding can help you break through your fear of the interview to build your courage for facing its hazards. Flooding can be broken into three basic steps:

1. Imagine that you are in an interview.
2. Try to make your palms sweaty (think of the toughest question the interviewer could ask).
3. Notice that you do not have the fear.

When you channel your fear of interviews, you will feel courage—and courage is better than self-confidence. Self-confidence is an attitude that can be swiftly shattered by one unexpected question. Courage means you have already confronted these dangers in your mind, and you're prepared to use all of your skills to overcome them.

KEEP A REIN ON POSITIVE FEELINGS

Negative feelings, such as fear, can be harnessed to help you meet the challenge of the interview; positive feelings can contribute energy directly to this task. The problem is that, like uncontrolled negative feelings, positive emotions can be self-reinforcing—that is, they can feed on themselves and spiral out of control.

In normal, everyday life, we perform best when we balance our positive and negative emotions. We let good feelings steer us into new opportunities and enterprises, and we let our fear and the memory of pain stop us from blundering into great danger.

Joy

It may seem strange to think of joy as something to avoid. But in an interview, it is usually an expression of relief in anticipation of leaving a bad situation, and this can be dangerous. Excessive joy can tip the interviewer to any of several facts about you that don't necessarily help your case.

Perhaps you feel joy because you felt like a slave in your old job. That's understandable. But why did you stay there so long? Are you indecisive? Are your skills less than good enough to get another job readily? Do you have an abnormal need for security, prestige, money? Was it a dictatorial boss, a poor working environment, boring work that made your job miserable—or could it have been you? Do you somehow need to be unhappy? Does the joy signify something else, like the spouse you're going to dump as soon as you get the new job? Excessive joy can invite an interviewer to speculate about you, and not favorably.

Maybe you're letting your career dreams get the better of your practical side. Some of my early jobs were not terribly interesting; I remember being preoccupied with what time I got off work. One time in my 20s I became very interested in early retirement—the ultimate way to get off early. But I was so excited when I did leave one of these boring jobs that I didn't exercise self-discipline; I neglected my early retirement strategy. My short-term joy about getting off work interfered with my ability to develop a long-term plan. Good feelings blocked productive action.

Job stress and alienation can also create unrealistic dreams of a second career. After all, one wants to leave with dignity intact, not being walked out the front door and dropped at the curb. Many such dreamers retire young with great aspirations. Relieved to be out of a disappointing career, they may have a general idea of what they want to do but fail to focus their energies toward developing new opportunities. When the intoxicating joy of relief becomes the thing itself, its energy is not channeled into an effective search plan.

I remember interviewing one candidate who was so relaxed that he seemed not to care whether he got the job or not. At one point he said, "I've got $50,000 in the bank and no debts. I've never felt so free in my life. I should buy my Harley and ride into the sunset!"

I thought to myself, This guy has no idea of how fast he can go broke. His $50,000 would have lasted him two years at best. After that, he'd never find a job paying what he could earn today. He was so happy to be "rich and free" that he failed to realize the value of his career.

Channel your joy into a practical strategy, a design for your future. Then it becomes a productive joy, the joy of anticipation and practical optimism, based on your vision of a job that helps you become who you want to be.

Confidence

Confidence makes you more sure-footed, more eloquent, more polished—less likely to embarrass yourself in an interview. But confidence can work against you, too.

I know an expert on human resources management who is very capable and experienced in selection, compensation, job analysis, organization development, and training. Her credentials, and her confidence in her abilities, are so strong that, paradoxically, they have kept her from getting jobs that matched her skills. Less qualified interviewers saw her confidence and skill as a threat, not a resource, and would hide her from other decision makers. When she became aware of this, she modified her interview strategy. Now she avoids discussing some of her strongest skills until she can assess the experience level of the interviewer. She gives high-level responses and shows strong confidence only when she knows the interviewer can handle it.

Your confidence can especially work against you if the interviewer perceives it as arrogance. Before you decide this point doesn't apply to you, remember that you are not the best judge of how the interviewer sees you. I have never heard a job candidate recognize arrogance as a reason a job was not offered. Arrogant people do not think of themselves as arrogant; they see themselves as decisive leaders with proven track records. If you think of yourself as confident, you should assume that some interviewers will consider you arrogant. Try to eliminate that perception before it happens.

You can reduce your chances of sounding arrogant by carefully managing how you use the word "I." This is not easy. Many interviewers will want to know exactly what you did in a particular situation, so you cannot altogether avoid the first person singular. But you can develop alternate speech patterns to describe your actions. Instead of saying, "This is what I did . . ." use a phrase such as "My contribution was . . ." Rather than "I told them to . . ." say, "The suggestion was . . ."

Overconfidence is the stuff of which comedy and tragedy are made. When you feel good about yourself, you may assume that you can just be yourself in your interviews without preparing to showcase your skills. You may forget how much competition there is for good jobs. Still worse, you may allow your confidence to justify a wait-and-see attitude. Although confidence can be a great ally in your interviews, it can also lead to complacency about developing your own strategy and following through on it.

HARNESS YOUR EMOTIONAL ENERGY

Naturally, because of what you have riding on the outcome, you'll come into an interview emotionally loaded. But you can use that emotional energy to your advantage—by redirecting it, or channeling it, in positive ways. Been let down too often? Turn that disappointment around and transform it into determination not to let it happen again. Anxiety? Let it drive you to prepare yourself for the interview; you'll gain an amazing amount of confidence if you know the answers in advance. Anger? Don't get mad at slackers and weirdos, get mad at that unemployment line; resolve to stay out of it. Joy? Sure, you're ecstatic about dumping that old job, but don't get giddy, get focused.

The best place to focus all that emotional energy is in positive steps to get ready for any eventuality in the interview. That's what this part of the book is about. The next four chapters will show you practical ways to identify and catalog your skills, match them with benefits for your potential employer, state them in a form that helps the interviewer come to positive conclusions about you, and anticipate tough questions about things you'd rather not talk about.

CHAPTER 5

PROFILE
YOUR
SKILLS

One of the best psychologists I have ever known was a master at coaching clients on self-assessment. He didn't talk very much; he rarely offered his opinion; he never told a client what to do. He simply asked good questions. I called him the "Velvet Hammer."

The questions he asked seemed to fall into four categories—as though demonstrating the four different interviewing styles we discussed earlier. But behind each of the questions he asked, there was a clear objective. He always knew what he wanted to learn about a person.

- As a gut-feel interviewer relying on impressions, he would try to find out, How do you make other people feel? To what extent does your first impression help or hurt you? Do you portray yourself as you really are, or do you maintain a façade? To what extent do you have a positive impact on others? What's your approach in making people like you?

- As a trait interviewer interested in your personality traits, he'd want to know, What are your best and worst characteristics? How do you define yourself? Are you more aggressive and driven, or more relaxed and cool? What is your relationship with yourself? How high is your self-esteem? Are you more driven by your want-tos or your ought-tos?

- As a conversational interviewer concerned with your work-related values, he might want to learn, What is important to you? How do your principles reflect a commitment to human dignity? Which of your principles conflict with those of society? What do you value in your relationships? How do you assess your worth, your skills, your achievements?

- As a behavioral-based interviewer looking for evidence of your job qualifications in your past behavior, he would ask questions like these: Give me an example of your number one skill at work. Tell me about a time when you used it well. Describe a time when you learned from a mistake. Tell me about a situation in which you were asked to solve a problem that others couldn't.

You will use each of these categories of questions as you profile your skills. This will help you get ready to answer questions asked by any interviewer. But you can anticipate turning all of your skill profiles into specific examples of times when you used your skills, regardless of the focus of the question.

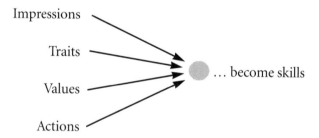

Impressions

Traits

Values

Actions

... become skills

KNOW THYSELF

In writing this book, I asked several people to pick one question that the Velvet Hammer might ask them and answer it. It was an intense exercise. Many were surprised at the request and reluctant to answer. However, with encouragement and discussion of the questions, each person came up with an answer, followed by a lot of explanation and more questions. The turnabout from reticence to an overeagerness to explain was typical. It showed just how interested most people are in talking about themselves.

Unfortunately, your interest in self-appraisal is usually not shared by interviewers; they want to draw their own conclusions about you, based on your answers to their questions. After all, if the interviewer asks you whether you work well with others, would you answer no? Astute interviewers ask you questions that make it difficult for you to be casual in talking about yourself. They want the "truth" about you, without frills.

Your main objective, of course, is to communicate your real qualifications to the interviewer. In this respect, your needs coincide with those of the organization. But to arrive at a clear understanding of your skills, you need to define yourself first in terms of your first impressions, traits, and values, the way a gut-feel, trait, or conversational interviewer might. Then you will assess your technical and performance skills in preparation for a behavioral-based interviewer. With this self-assessment firmly in mind, you will have a foundation for identifying exactly what skills you have that can be translated into benefits for your potential employer.

PROFILE YOUR FIRST IMPRESSIONS, TRAITS, AND VALUES

This chapter contains exercises that are designed to help you define yourself in terms of four basic questions. In this section, you will deal with, What impressions do you generate? What are your traits? and What is important to you? In the next section you will be asked to define yourself in terms of What can you do? Take time to respond to each of these exercises by rating yourself or writing out your answer. This will help bring your self-definition into focus. However, if your learning style is more reflective, you can read each exercise, think through your answers, and make brief notes on your thoughts.

You can ask people who know you well to complete the forms, then compare your self-appraisal with what others say about you. The best profile is one that closely matches the interviewer's beliefs about what would be a good fit for the job. Since this is almost always impossible to know, your best strategy is to convert each of the impressions you generate into a description of a skill that will help you do the job well.

Remember, the ultimate goal of these exercises is to relate your impressions, traits, values, and past behavior to your skills. The purpose of this chapter is to help you profile your skills as you prepare for interviews. It is not designed to guide your personal growth, but to help you describe to an interviewer what you can do on the job. In the interview, you should emphasize your past actions that showcase your skills; how others perceive you, your traits, and your values is important, but secondary.

PROFILE YOUR SKILLS

The behavioral-based interviewer will want to find out what you can do by assessing what you have done in specific instances in the past. For this reason, the first step in profiling your skills is to overcome your impulse to define yourself in generalities. The way you see yourself is so loaded with emotion that you can forget that your main task is preparing yourself to succeed in an interview. How you feel about yourself can interfere with the logical, analytical process of profiling your skills, answering the What can you do? question.

There are two general types of work skills that you need to assess in yourself before taking a behavioral-based interview: performance skills and technical skills.

- *Performance skills* are work habits that you can transfer between jobs. Often learned early in life, they apply to many different kinds of work and reflect broad attitudes and beliefs about how a job should be done. These skills may be enhanced by education, but their foundations are set in life experiences. Leadership, teamwork, and communication are types of performance skills.

- *Technical skills* include being able to perform a specific task in the performance of a job. Such skills are typically taught in colleges or vocational schools—and, in some cases, company training programs. Some technical skills include the knowledge needed to do a job well. For example,

---

COACH'S TIP

Try to be objective when you describe your impressions, traits, values, and skills. Balance your choices so that you develop a representative picture of your positives and negatives. You can learn to be more objective about yourself by assessing alternately your strengths and weaknesses—giving yourself first what you feel to be a high rating, then a low rating, and so on.

you may know how to apply statistical techniques to identify work-flow problems. Other technical skills involve using the tools and equipment needed to do the job. Computer programming, driving, and welding are technical skills.

WHAT IMPRESSIONS DO YOU GENERATE?

Here is a list of impressions that describe how a gut-feel interviewer might react to you. Select the box on each continuum that best describes the first impression you make on others. Then review your assessment in order to better understand your first impression.

People who know me well would say that the first impression I generate is—

	More like this impression	Somewhat in this direction	About like most people	Somewhat in this direction	More like this impression	
ATTITUDE						
Closed	❏	❏	❏	❏	❏	Open
Insecure	❏	❏	❏	❏	❏	Confident
Distant	❏	❏	❏	❏	❏	Friendly
Reluctant	❏	❏	❏	❏	❏	Cooperative
APPEARANCE						
Unconcerned	❏	❏	❏	❏	❏	Professional
Soiled	❏	❏	❏	❏	❏	Immaculate
Slouched	❏	❏	❏	❏	❏	Erect
Unkempt	❏	❏	❏	❏	❏	Well-groomed
MANNERISMS						
Nervous	❏	❏	❏	❏	❏	Poised
Leaning back	❏	❏	❏	❏	❏	Leaning forward
Indirect	❏	❏	❏	❏	❏	Face-to-face
Slow	❏	❏	❏	❏	❏	Energetic
PREPARATION						
Late	❏	❏	❏	❏	❏	Punctual
Disorganized	❏	❏	❏	❏	❏	Detailed

WHAT ARE YOUR TRAITS?

Below is a list of traits that can be used to sketch a rough outline of your personality. For each trait listed, select the box on the scale that best describes how you think others see you. Then evaluate your self-assessment in light of your interview objectives.

People who know me well would say that I am—

	More like this trait	Somewhat in this direction	About like most people	Somewhat in this direction	More like this trait	
INTERPERSONAL						
Humble	❏	❏	❏	❏	❏	Assertive
Reserved	❏	❏	❏	❏	❏	Outgoing
Serious	❏	❏	❏	❏	❏	Enthusiastic
AGREEABLENESS						
Questioning	❏	❏	❏	❏	❏	Accepting
Self-directing	❏	❏	❏	❏	❏	Conforming
Independent	❏	❏	❏	❏	❏	Dependent
Suspicious	❏	❏	❏	❏	❏	Trusting
EMOTIONALITY						
Stable	❏	❏	❏	❏	❏	Changeable
Relaxed	❏	❏	❏	❏	❏	Tense
Confident	❏	❏	❏	❏	❏	Anxious
Resilient	❏	❏	❏	❏	❏	Fragile
CONSCIENTIOUSNESS						
Shrewd	❏	❏	❏	❏	❏	Principled
Lax	❏	❏	❏	❏	❏	Detail-oriented
Creative	❏	❏	❏	❏	❏	Practical
OPENNESS TO EXPERIENCE						
Steady	❏	❏	❏	❏	❏	Changing
Closed	❏	❏	❏	❏	❏	Open
Standard	❏	❏	❏	❏	❏	Innovative

WHAT ARE YOUR VALUES?

Below is a list of values that can be used to describe the principles and broad motivations that guide your actions in your work. For each value listed, select the box on the scale that best describes how you think others see you. Then review your findings in order to profile your values.

People who know me well would say that my values are—

	More like this value	Somewhat in this direction	About like most people	Somewhat in this direction	More like this value	
SOCIAL VALUES						
Uninvolved	☐	☐	☐	☐	☐	Supportive
Independent	☐	☐	☐	☐	☐	Relationship-oriented
Few friends	☐	☐	☐	☐	☐	Numerous friends
Self-directed	☐	☐	☐	☐	☐	Other-directed
WORK VALUES						
Need to enjoy	☐	☐	☐	☐	☐	Need to achieve
Avoid high standards	☐	☐	☐	☐	☐	Set high standards
Pleasure-oriented	☐	☐	☐	☐	☐	Task-oriented
Complete easy tasks	☐	☐	☐	☐	☐	Master difficult tasks
Short work time	☐	☐	☐	☐	☐	Long hours
Spontaneous	☐	☐	☐	☐	☐	Organized
Impulsive	☐	☐	☐	☐	☐	Disciplined
Lack of goals	☐	☐	☐	☐	☐	Clear goals
Spends resources	☐	☐	☐	☐	☐	Saves resources
Frivolous	☐	☐	☐	☐	☐	Frugal
CHANGE ORIENTATION						
Scheduled work	☐	☐	☐	☐	☐	Changeable schedule
Stay at home	☐	☐	☐	☐	☐	Travel
Predictable activities	☐	☐	☐	☐	☐	New activities
Structured work	☐	☐	☐	☐	☐	Unstructured work
COMMITMENT TO PRINCIPLE						
Use situational ethics	☐	☐	☐	☐	☐	Follow principles
Accept customs	☐	☐	☐	☐	☐	Set personal standards
Expedient	☐	☐	☐	☐	☐	Ethical
"Spin" ideas	☐	☐	☐	☐	☐	Honest opinions
Ignore deception	☐	☐	☐	☐	☐	Confront deception

YEAH-BUT

I know that I don't have all the right skills for today's workplace.

COACH'S COMEBACK

You do have the right skills for some jobs. If you can speak reasonably well, read, and write, you have the basic skills required for many jobs. However, you may be asking this question because you're afraid you can't learn other skills that you need. Let me help you make your fear work for you. Answer this question for yourself: "Why don't I use my skills assessment as a starting point for future learning?"

The following classifications of work skills were developed from the SCANS project, initiated by the U.S. Department of Labor.[1] Leaders from education, business, and industry identified the types of skills that were important for future performance. Each of these categories can be used to help you define your performance and technical skills before the interviewer asks you about them.

Performance Skills

Performance skills are often called "competencies." Many of today's more progressive organizations have lists of competencies they use to develop performance-skill questions for interviews. These competencies reflect the performance skills that the interviewer looks for in your background. When preparing for your interview, you should anticipate how you will answer a variety of performance-skill questions.

Before you review the following list of competencies, consider the following questions about your own performance skills:[2]

- What experiences have taught you important work habits?
- How are your successes at work linked to your competencies?
- Which of your mistakes at work link to your competencies?
- How do your work goals relate to improving your competencies?

Adaptability

Shows Resilience: Rebounds from conflict and difficult situations; treats a negative experience as a learning opportunity; responds to time pressures and interpersonal conflicts with problem-solving actions; withholds negative comments and emotional outbursts; is respectful of others, even under pressure.

Accommodates Changes: Responds open-mindedly to change initiatives, looking for ways to help the organization; offers opinions about changes in a supportive manner; follows team agreement on changes in ways that help their effectiveness; resists changes that may be unsafe or illegal.

Interpersonal

Participates in Teamwork: Works cooperatively and contributes ideas, suggestions, and effort to the group; communicates acceptance or rejection of team commitments; does not talk about team members negatively in their absence; is willing to confront team performance problems.

Displays Leadership: Communicates thoughts, feelings, and ideas to justify a position; encourages, persuades, or otherwise motivates individuals or groups; challenges existing procedures, policies, or authority responsibly.

Manages Conflict: Expresses opinions directly and clearly without abuse or manipulation; listens to the opinions and feelings of others and demonstrates understanding by restating them; communicates disagreement to persons in authority as necessary; accepts negative feedback as a way to learn; negotiates agreements to resolve differences.

Accepts Differences: Works effectively with individuals from diverse backgrounds; behaves professionally and supportively when working with men and women from a variety of ethnic, social, and educational backgrounds; avoids using stereotypes when dealing with others; may correct others on the use of slurs and negative comments about diverse groups.

Provides Service: Works and communicates with clients and customers to satisfy their expectations; adapts one's own needs and objectives to help others reach their objectives; presents difficult information in an attention-getting and persuasive manner.

Work Habits

Exhibits Integrity: Gathers and uses information in ways that respect confidentiality, business ethics, and organizational secrets; makes truthful comments based on verifiable information; avoids using rumor, gossip, and subjective opinions in decision making; is sensitive to perceived integrity issues; produces complete and accurate written documents.

Manages Oneself: Uses standard operating procedures and work instructions to guide one's own actions without supervision; selects relevant, goal-related activities and ranks them in order of importance; allocates time to activities, and understands, prepares, and follows schedules; periodically makes decisions that are consistent with the job mission but not guided by policy and procedures.

Motivates Oneself and Others: Starts work oneself and gets others started working; commits to a plan of action and shows a willingness to work hard and long to achieve measurable results; completes tasks quickly; competes productively against oneself, time allocations, and others.

Follows Procedures: Understands, follows, and encourages others to follow prescribed policies and procedures, even when it is inconvenient to do so; improves performance by telling others where policies and procedures interfere with productivity.

Technical Skills

Your interview may include questions about your technical skills. Depending on the type of job you are seeking, these questions may be very specific about the technical details of your work, or they may concern only your general knowledge and skills. In either case, it is important for your interview preparation to include the general areas of your technical skills.

The following competencies are general areas of technical skills. You must define them for your line of work.

Resources

Allocates Money: Uses or prepares budgets; makes cost and revenue forecasts; keeps detailed records to track budget performance; makes appropriate adjustments.

Allocates Material and Facility Resources: Acquires, stores, and distributes materials, supplies, parts, equipment, space, or final products in order to make the best use of them.

Allocates Human Resources: Assesses knowledge and skills and distributes work accordingly; evaluates performance; provides feedback.

Information

Acquires and Evaluates Information: Identifies need for data; obtains data from existing sources or creates data; evaluates relevance and accuracy of data.

Organizes and Maintains Information: Organizes, processes, and maintains written or computerized records and other forms of information in a systematic fashion.

Interprets and Communicates Information: Selects and analyzes information and communicates the results to others using oral, written, graphic, pictorial, or multimedia methods.

Uses Computers to Process Information: Employs computers to acquire, organize, analyze, and communicate information.

Systems

Understands Systems: Knows how social, organizational, and technological systems work and operates effectively within them.

Monitors and Corrects Performance: Distinguishes trends; predicts impact of actions on system operations; diagnoses deviations in the function of a system/organization; takes necessary action to correct performance.

Improves and Designs Systems: Makes suggestions to modify existing systems to improve products or services, and develops new or alternative systems.

Technology

Selects Technology: Judges which set of procedures, tools, or machines, including computers and their programs, will produce the desired results; helps others learn.

Applies Technology to Task: Understands the overall intent and the proper procedures for setting up and operating machines, including computers and their programming systems.

Maintains and Troubleshoots Technology: Prevents, identifies, or solves problems in machines, computers, and other technologies.

YEAH-BUT

I already know myself pretty well. Why should I bother with all this self-assessment?

COACH'S COMEBACK

Okay, let's say that you do know yourself well. But you have never been at this exact point in your life before. The odds are that your skills have evolved since your last self-assessment. Also, the job market is changing so fast that it is logical for you to reposition what you do know about yourself in terms of the performance skills and technical skills that today's employers look for. Then you will be better able to construct honest, specific answers to questions on a variety of new and emerging selection criteria.

Your Skill Profile

Now that you have reviewed the performance skill and technical skill definitions, you can assess how strong or how weak you are in each of the skills. Plot
your self-assessment on the chart ("Your Skill Profile") to get a graphic repre-
sentation of your skills.

Remember that you are drawing this skill profile to give yourself—and no
one else—an accurate picture of your strengths and weaknesses. Make it as
useful as possible.

Keep in mind that technical skills are described earlier in more general
terms than the specific skills that you will offer an employer. This list should
help you identify the general categories of technical skills in your type of work.
However, you should define more specifically each of the skills that you use in
your work.

YOUR SKILL PROFILE

Below is a list of performance and technical skills. Rate your skill level in each category by circling the appropriate point. Then connect the circled points with a line to construct your skill profile.

Try not to rate all your skills as simply high or low, but try to distribute them across all levels. Here is a general rule to follow. For the performance skills and for the technical skills allow yourself

2–3 ones or sevens

3–4 twos or sixes

4–5 threes or fives

5–6 fours

This will give you a range of skill ratings that will help you to decide how to prepare your answers. Your stronger self-ratings will be used in chapter 10 in formulating SHARE answers. Your weaker ratings will be used in chapter 11 where you will learn to deal with "killer" questions.

Performance Skills	1 (low skill)	2	3	4	5	6	7 (high skill)
ADAPTABILITY							
Shows Resilience	•	•	•	•	•	•	•
Accommodates Changes	•	•	•	•	•	•	•
INTERPERSONAL							
Participates in Teamwork	•	•	•	•	•	•	•
Displays Leadership	•	•	•	•	•	•	•
Manages Conflict	•	•	•	•	•	•	•
Accepts Differences	•	•	•	•	•	•	•
Provides Service	•	•	•	•	•	•	•
WORK HABITS							
Exhibits Integrity	•	•	•	•	•	•	•
Manages Oneself	•	•	•	•	•	•	•
Motivates Self and Others	•	•	•	•	•	•	•
Follows Procedures	•	•	•	•	•	•	•

Technical Skills	1 (low skill)	2	3	4	5	6	7 (high skill)
RESOURCES							
Allocates Money	•	•	•	•	•	•	•
Allocates Material/ Facility Resources	•	•	•	•	•	•	•
Allocates Human Resources	•	•	•	•	•	•	•
INFORMATION							
Acquires/Evaluates Information	•	•	•	•	•	•	•
Organizes/Maintains Information	•	•	•	•	•	•	•
Interprets/Communicates Information	•	•	•	•	•	•	•
Uses Computers to Process Information	•	•	•	•	•	•	•
SYSTEMS							
Understands Systems	•	•	•	•	•	•	•
Monitors/Corrects Performance	•	•	•	•	•	•	•
Improves/Designs Systems	•	•	•	•	•	•	•
TECHNOLOGY							
Selects Technology	•	•	•	•	•	•	•
Applies Technology to Task	•	•	•	•	•	•	•
Maintains/Troubleshoots Technology	•	•	•	•	•	•	•

MY SKILL SUMMARY

The most important impressions I generate are _____

_____.

In light of the impressions I tend to generate, I can say that I am able to
1. _____
2. _____
3. _____

My most important traits for my work are _____

_____.

In light of my traits, I can say that I am able to
1. _____
2. _____
3. _____

My most important values for my work are _____

_____.

In light of my values, I can say that I am able to
1. _____
2. _____
3. _____

My most important performance skills for my work are _____

_____.

In light of my performance skills, I can say that I am able to
1. _____
2. _____
3. _____

My most important technical skills for my work are _____

_____.

In light of my technical skills, I can say that I am able to
1. _____
2. _____
3. _____

SUMMARIZE YOUR SKILLS

Having identified yourself in terms of the impression you make on others, your personality traits, your work values, and your technical and performance skills, your next move will be to summarize them. This exercise will give you a clearer overall portrait of yourself as a potentially valuable employee that you can sell as a package to the potential employer.

A skill can be thought of as an action that can be seen or heard as it is being performed. It is learnable, transferable, and potentially job related. Thus, you can describe a skill as something that you are "able to" do.

After reviewing your ratings on the previous exercises, summarize your job strengths by completing the form, "My Skill Summary." Think of what you are able to do as a consequence of each way of defining yourself—impressions, traits, values, and skills. Write your self-appraisal in the blanks provided. This will help you translate your self-definition into marketable employee skills.

TAILOR YOUR RESPONSES

Your success as a candidate will be greatly influenced by the level to which you can honestly spotlight parts of your self-definition that relate to each interviewer's needs. Using the different interview styles we discussed in chapter 3, you can make an informed guess on the types of needs interviewers have.

- The gut-feel interviewer makes a decision based on how good he or she feels about you. You should highlight the parts of your self-definition that line up with this interviewer's experiences and values. Respond to warmth with human interest stories. When you field specific questions, maintain a serious demeanor with a "just business" professionalism.

- The trait interviewer wants to find out about your personality traits, such as enthusiasm, versatility, and sensitivity. Here it is desirable for you to describe yourself in terms of the general characteristics you have that can be of value to the interviewer.

- The conversational interviewer wants to find out about you as a person—the whole you, including the principles that guide your actions and your beliefs about the right way to handle situations. Emphasize the parts of your self-definition that reflect your values and beliefs.

- The behavioral-based interviewer wants to assess your job-related skills. Your answers should focus on describing times when you used these skills—actual events that show how your skills helped get the job done.

You should by now have a clearer picture of your strengths as well as areas where you need improvement. The next chapter takes you on a big step toward communicating your qualifications in the interview. You will present each of your marketable skills and its corresponding benefit to the employer in the form of a spoken skill-benefit statement. And you will practice making these statements aloud, as you will when you talk with the interviewer in person or on the telephone.

CHAPTER 6

PREPARE
SKILL-BENEFIT
STATEMENTS

When you are going for an interview, remember that the interviewer is a buyer, representing an organization that needs someone who can both provide a set of skills and apply them to accomplish one or more goals. You are the seller, and your immediate task in the interview is to let the buyer know what skills you have and how those skills can benefit the organization.

What are your skills? Are they merely knowledge, things you know how to do in theory but have never done? Are they experience, combining theoretical and practical knowledge? Do you have skills you are not aware of? Do you have skills that you alone are aware of? Or are your abilities mostly a matter of charm and personality, with little practical knowledge? These are philosophical questions that bear on your self-esteem, your usefulness to others, your integrity, your popularity—and thus your value to an employer.

For the interview, however, you must set aside such concerns and address the question that is paramount in the interviewer's mind: What can you do for us? To answer this question, you should respond with a set of skill-benefit statements.

In chapter 5, you catalogued your strengths and connected them with implied actions in a series of written statements. In this chapter you will practice putting together each of your skills and its benefits for your potential employer in the form of a two-part statement. And you will begin to rehearse for the interview by reciting these skill-benefit statements aloud.

HOW TO MAKE A SKILL-BENEFIT STATEMENT

The way you communicate your value to the interviewer is to convert your skill profile into a set of skill-benefit statements. Each statement consists of two parts: (1) a basic description of a skill that you have, and (2) a summary of the benefits that the skill can generate—in sum, your value to the organization.

A skill-benefit statement begins with a phrase that describes your skill:

"I can instruct and coach on the use of laser calibration instruments."

Note that the skill description uses "can," a word that emphasizes actions that can be taken. This is a stronger way of stating your skills than using such phrasing as "I know how to instruct and coach on the use of laser calibration instruments." Although they mean much the same thing, "can" conveys a more positive attitude and greater confidence.

Then, to complete your skill-benefit statement, simply add an implication to the skill description:

"So I could begin training your people on the day I start to work for you."

COACH'S TIP

A skill-benefit statement encourages you to talk in a way that combines "I can" with "able to." For example: "I can program your inventory records so that you will be able to reorder supplies at just the right time."

THE BENEFITS OF YOUR IMPRESSIONS, TRAITS, AND VALUES

In the first part of "Your Skill Summary" in chapter 5, you connected your most significant first impressions, traits, and values with particular skills. In this exercise, develop a skill-benefit statement for each category, describing the implications of each skill in terms of a benefit to a potential employer. Then practice saying it aloud.

My impression/trait/value/skill is: _____

Skill-Benefit Statement: I can _____,
  (skill)
so I will be able to _____
  (benefit to the employer)
_____.

Note that the implication expresses what the person will be able to do for the employer. It makes this statement in a way that assumes that a job offer will be made. It says, ". . . on the day I start to work for you," not ". . . if I start to work for you." The phrase reflects confidence, as it assumes that a job offer will be forthcoming.

Avoid Ego Trips

There's a big difference between making skill-benefit statements and bragging. A braggart is quite capable of self-entertainment—perhaps even forgetting about the interviewer. If you find yourself rattling off all the wonderful things you have learned how to do in your life, you're probably bragging. You've lost sight of what the interviewer wants: information needed to make a good hiring decision.

Pay close attention to what the interviewer asks you about a specific skill. Focus your answer on the value the organization can derive from your skill. A well-framed skill-benefit statement helps the interviewer make a good decision for the organization, for you, and for other candidates.

You may be better off not mentioning some of the skills you are most proud of. They may seem important to you, but if they don't answer the employer's needs, you're wasting the interviewer's time by talking about them. Some of the

YEAH-BUT

I've always been told to avoid saying "I" too much. Most of your examples suggest the use of "I."

COACH'S COMEBACK

You're right. Using "I" too much may give the interviewer the impression that you have a big ego. However, for these exercises I have asked you to use the word "I" on purpose to help you identify exactly what you have to offer. Once you have done this, you can use your skill-benefit statements as part of your past work experience, which can include recognition of team efforts and the resources that others made available to you.

skills you value most highly may even seem frivolous to the interviewer; do many organizations need the services of a bass guitar player? A skilled weight watcher? A ham radio operator? It's better to emphasize the skills the interviewer asks you about, regardless of the ones that you value most highly.

SAMPLE SKILL-BENEFIT STATEMENTS

"I can work with difficult people, so I will have no problem fitting into any situation you place me in."

"I can develop an up-to-date policy manual that is consistent with EEO, ADA, OFPC, and OSHA regulations, so I'll be able to develop your manual in a timely and professional manner."

"I can provide sensitive patient care in an AIDS pediatric unit, so I can be an effective member of the team by next Monday."

"By running the digital lathe on the night shift, I can help you maintain production with little down time."

"With my ability and experience installing and repairing DOS-based LAN systems, I can get your computers talking to each other in less than twenty days."

"I can use key financial ratios to develop a series of pro formas that will enable you to reduce your line of credit and free up cash."

Above all, don't use the interviewer as a captive audience for the story of your wonderfulness as a person. Describe your skills and how you can use them for the interviewer's organization, not what you are like as a person. After all is said and done, today's employer is more interested in how fast and how well you can use a skill than in how much your co-workers will admire you.

HOW TO USE SKILL-BENEFIT STATEMENTS

By itself, formulating skill-benefit statements is only one step in preparing for your interview. It is not enough simply to walk in and mechanically recite a canned listing of your abilities and their value to the employer.

I once knew a salesperson who would hammer potential customers with benefits. His presentation was fast, specific, and to the point. There was no doubt what the salesperson thought of his product. However, his sales technique seemed directed mostly at his own needs rather than those of the customer.

Think of how you carry on a conversation with a friend. Whatever the subject matter, you don't simply throw out random observations, or interrupt with remarks that have nothing to do with what your friend is talking about—at

---

"I can develop a marketing plan, write ad copy around it, and develop a quality sales training program. So you can expect me to produce immediate results in the marketing department."

"I can make money. Some people just know how to make money. Within a month on the job my billings will exceed my salary."

"I have the knack of getting people to like me. Give me your most difficult group and I'll have them doing a reasonable level of work within two weeks."

"I can reengineer a work group by analyzing work processes and finding bottlenecks. This means that on the job you can expect me to have improved performance in record time."

"I can type eighty words per minute. I can take shorthand. I can file with absolute accuracy. I can make your job easier for you."

PERFORMANCE AND TECHNICAL SKILL BENEFITS

Review the performance and technical skill definitions in chapter 5. Check the skills below that apply to you. Then develop a skill-benefit statement for each, using the following format as a guide.

I can _____,

so on this job I will be able to _____.

Performance Skills

ADAPTABILITY

    Shows Resilience   ❏

    Accommodates Changes   ❏

INTERPERSONAL

    Participates in Teamwork   ❏

    Displays Leadership   ❏

    Manages Conflict   ❏

    Accepts Differences   ❏

    Provides Service   ❏

WORK HABITS

    Exhibits Integrity   ❏

    Manages Oneself   ❏

    Motivates Self and Others   ❏

    Follows Procedures   ❏

---

least, not if you expect to remain friends. You follow the flow of conversation, interjecting your own comments where appropriate.

A good interview should be as mutually satisfying as a good conversation. You should pay careful attention to what the interviewer is saying and, with appropriate timing, weave your skill-benefit statements into the conversation. Just as in any friendly conversation, strive for honesty and modesty. Base your delivery and emphasis on the importance of the topic, as indicated by the interviewer's question. The skill with which you address the needs of the behavioral-based interviewer will also make a good impression on the gut-feel interviewer, the trait interviewer, and the conversational interviewer.

Technical Skills

RESOURCES

Allocates Money	❏
Allocates Material/Facility Resources	❏
Allocates Human Resources	❏

INFORMATION

Acquires/Evaluates Information	❏
Organizes/Maintains Information	❏
Interprets/Communicates Information	❏
Uses Computers to Process Information	❏

SYSTEMS

Understands Systems	❏
Monitors/Corrects Performance	❏
Improves/Designs Systems	❏

TECHNOLOGY

Selects Technology	❏
Applies Technology to Task	❏
Maintains/Troubleshoots Technology	❏

It is important for you to practice saying these skill-benefit statements aloud. It's a lot like rehearsing for a speech or a play; the sound of your voice becomes more familiar to you, and you can picture yourself actually saying these things to the interviewer. You gain confidence.

There is, however, an important difference between practicing skill-benefit statements aloud and learning your lines in a play. In the interview, you don't know exactly what the interviewer is going to ask. You must be ready for anything. Therefore, it is the format that you're practicing, not the exact wording you'll use. You need to get comfortable with the process of framing your qualifications in the form of skill-benefit statements—not memorizing an unchanging script.

Adapt to the Interview

Just as your tone, emphasis, and attitude will naturally vary in the course of a lively conversation, you should use a variety of techniques to present your skill-benefit statements as you respond to the interviewer's questions.

Sprinkle benefits. Season the interview like a gourmet dish by offering a range of skills:

- you're an expert on developing biodegradable plastics;

- you can supervise large teams of researchers in successful product development efforts; what's more,

- you are an experienced research writer and can help the advertising department write copy describing the benefits of your products.

This approach is helpful in a panel interview; offering a variety of benefits raises your chances of mentioning at least one skill that will interest each interviewer. It is especially useful when you don't know very much about the job you will be doing. Sometimes even the interviewer doesn't know exactly what your job will be; using the sprinkle approach, you'll cover so many skills that some are sure to be appropriate for whatever the job turns out to be.

Target benefits. If you know in advance what the job involves, you can prepare honest, accurate skill-benefit statements that match the job description, emphasizing the parts of your skill profile that are most relevant to the position. You can emphasize a specific area of technical experience, your international business experience, or your ability to work in ambiguous situations. Target specific performance-skill areas, too; if the interviewer's organization is phasing in team-based management or production techniques, emphasize your experience with teams in other work situations.

Compare and contrast. Whenever you can do so without sounding negative, communicate your skill level by comparing or contrasting your work with the good work of others. Show your breadth: "I can perform most of the stress-distribution analyses that Ph.D. engineers did on my last job." Describe an improvement that you made: "I used my knowledge of personnel systems to develop the first performance-based compensation program at Grace Hospital." It's best not to sound critical of your co-workers or your organization; remember, comparing your skills with a higher standard can only enhance them in the interviewer's eyes.

COULD DO VS. CAN DO

It is tempting to think that you can do something just because you understand how to do it. This is just not true. You may understand how to phrase the benefits you offer, but you should write them out in advance. Otherwise, the chances are that when it comes to the crunch, you won't be able to come up with skill-benefit statements that show the broad array of things that you can do.

You will find great value in writing out your skill-benefit statements. We asked several people to write skill-benefit statements and then comment on what they learned by doing so. Here are some of the things they said:

- "At first I couldn't write down more than four benefits. So I had lunch with some of my co-workers and they basically told me some skills I had that I didn't even know about."

- "It was pretty easy for me to do. I completed thirty-three skill-benefit statements for the categories that were relevant to my career. Then I revised my résumé to reflect a greater breadth of skills."

- "I got my mother to do it for herself. She has not worked out of the home for twenty-seven years. A lot of what she has done converted to skill statements."

- "I was surprised to see a big gap between what my values are and my 'can do' statements. It seems that I don't act on my values as much as I thought I did."

Show and tell. Bring a work sample to the interview and describe the skills you used in developing it. A program developer I once interviewed for a job at Behavioral Technology® brought several examples of her work. As we looked at what she had done, she described the steps that she had taken in developing the programs. When I asked technical questions, she replied with skill-benefit statements; these and her work samples showed me that she was skilled with development software and aware of the problems faced by a corporate trainer.

Share credit. Even though you need to impress the interviewer with your will and abilities, don't foster the impression that you see yourself as the single cause of your successes. Describe the opportunities you were given, then explain what you did to take advantage of them. Acknowledge the skills of the teams you worked with; allude to the synergy that resulted when you lent your skills to the team effort. Identify the important aspects of an organization's culture that helped mold and refine your skills, for the good of all. Giving ample credit to the source, recognize what you were taught by a mentor or teacher and describe the skill-benefit that grew from it.

Watch your body language. During the twenty years that I conducted selection interviews, I was usually more conscious of what candidates were saying than of their nonverbal signals. However, I did take notes on the body language and gestures that accompanied some of their answers. Recently, reviewing five years of my interview notes, I was astonished to see how many time I wrote down such comments as "hands to face" and "leaning forward." I now realize that my impressions of candidates were influenced by these nonverbal messages—and that most interviewers are similarly influenced, consciously or unconsciously. Moving one's hand to the face is a sign of discomfort or lack of confidence. Leaning forward and nodding affirmatively reflects pride and confidence. This suggests to me that when you make skill-benefit statements you should sit up and lean forward. Keep your hands away from your face; the table or your lap is a good place for them.

End with a benefit. A good conversation flows smoothly when one participant follows through on the last thing said by another. If you end your answer by stating a skill-benefit, you will increase the likelihood that the interviewer's next question will deal with your skill. This technique is especially good at steering the unstructured interviewer—the one without a list of prepared questions—to keep the interview focused on the skills to be assessed. But it will also help you deal with a structured interviewer by bringing to his attention additional topics that may help your case.

Each of these techniques is based on your ability to formulate a number of honest, accurate skill-benefit statements—a process you can begin by converting the skill profile you constructed in the last chapter to a series of brief statements that you can use as needed in your interviews.

PUTTING IT ALL TOGETHER

By completing this chapter, you have reached an important milestone in interview preparation. If you finished all the exercises, you now have several skill-benefit statements to use in selling your skills to the interviewer. This will make you a standout candidate. And—perhaps more important—you should have a better idea of what you have to offer. Having practiced stating aloud your skills and their associated benefits, you should have more confidence now that you can handle yourself in the interview. Your confidence will be self-evident; it will be real and honest, because it is based on your skills.

You now have the foundation you need to advance to a more thorough way of answering questions the interviewer asks you. In chapter 7, you'll learn how to invest your answers with more detail and experience by describing times when you actually used the skills that you've described in your skill-benefit statements. And you'll get more practice in describing your qualifications aloud.

CHAPTER 7

GET SPECIFIC WITH
SHARE ANSWERS

Storytelling is an ancient tradition, a way humans have of passing along experience and knowledge to others. In everyday conversations, we tell stories about ourselves—what situations we found ourselves in, who was there, what was said, how we felt, what we did, what happened after that. It is an economical and entertaining way of making contact with others, sharing our experiences, making sense of the world, justifying our actions.

In an interview, you are called upon to accomplish many of the same things. You are asked to talk about your knowledge, your skills with tools, your work habits—all the things that qualify you for the job. Unlike a casual conversation, however, the interview is a place to be specific, rather than general—to tell stories about yourself that highlight specific skills. To substantiate a particular technical or performance skill you have that qualifies you for the job, it is best to tell the interviewer about a situation in which you used that skill. Your story needs to include all the relevant details about the

> ### COACH'S TIP
>
> When you take the time to develop specific answers, you're doing more than simply preparing for specific questions. One of the biggest benefits you will get is confidence. Knowing what to say will make you comfortable and smooth in the interview.

situation, the hindrances, your actions, the results of your actions, and the outcome. And you need to show that you understand the larger meaning of your own experience.

But, you ask, how do I know what kind of interview to get ready for? How can I prepare to explain my skills to any interviewer when I haven't heard the kinds of questions that I will be asked? The answer is, it doesn't matter. Being prepared to give specific information will help you be successful in just about any interview, regardless of the approach that is used.

- A gut-feel interviewer, who usually doesn't ask for specific information, is more likely to be influenced by specific examples than by generalities.

- A trait interviewer will draw conclusions about your personal characteristics based on your examples of past behavior.

- A conversational interviewer will find it easy to build rapport when you are confident of your answers. In addition, your values will show through your actions.

- A behavioral-based interviewer wants to hear about your past actions and how you used your job-related skills.

As you can see, giving specific examples pays off for just about any type of interview.[1]

FORMULATING A SHARE ANSWER

Instead of talking about feelings, traits, and generalities in your answers, give candid, comprehensive examples of times when you used specific skills. The SHARE technique is an excellent guide for preparing these examples and showcasing your skills. A SHARE answer provides specific information on the situation, hindrances, actions, results, and evaluation of your example. Here's how it works:

Situation:	Begin by describing the situation in which you were operating.
Hindrances:	Describe any constraints or hindrances on your actions.
Actions:	Explain exactly what you did.
Results:	Describe the results that can be attributed to your actions.
Evaluation:	Summarize the example with a positive evaluation of your skill.

Using the SHARE technique, prepare fifteen to twenty examples, as honest and complete as you can, of times when you used different skills at work. This gives you time to survey your skills so you can be clear, accurate, and comfortable in the interview. Having several accurate answers on the tip of your tongue makes you better able to answer difficult questions. You will project your best image, rather than your nervous image.

Take special care to answer the exact question that was asked. This may seem so obvious as to be barely worth mentioning, but I've been astonished over the years at how often qualified, able candidates answer questions that weren't asked. Sometimes, of course, this means simply that they misunderstood, or are so nervous that they begin answering without taking time to think. But the perception that you aren't very good at listening or following instructions damages your chances of getting the job.

PRESENTING YOUR SHARE ANSWER

In my experience as an interviewer, candidates who give focused, specific, and relevant answers use some combination of these steps:

1. Listen carefully to the question, perhaps restating it to confirm your understanding.
2. Ask for clarification if necessary.
3. Look to the side and pause to think of an example that will answer the question.
4. Answer the question candidly and specifically, using the SHARE model.
5. Ask whether your answer addresses the question.

Don't follow these steps mechanically, as if you were programming your VCR; if you do, you'll end up sounding like a robot. Use common sense; be

---

YEAH-BUT

Is it really worth my time to do all this preparation? If I'm too prepared, my answers will sound canned.

COACH'S COMEBACK

Wrong! Preparing specific interview answers will take you only two hours or so—time that will make you a stronger competitor in your interviews. And it's not preparation that makes you sound "canned," it's *incomplete* preparation. In order to be really good in your interview, practice giving specific examples of your skills aloud until you feel comfortable doing it.

---

flexible. Practice using them to answer imaginary questions; become familiar with them; try out variations. Then, in the interview, let the interviewer's approach and the specific questions guide your answers.

Most interviewers will ask you ten to twenty questions in an hour. Each of your answers should use at least some components of the SHARE model. You may be tempted to ask the interviewer to reuse your answer to a previous question; resist the temptation. Each question you are asked gives you a new opportunity to communicate your fitness for the job, and each answer you give that relates to other questions helps your cause even more. Be prepared to give specific answers to many different interview questions, and use each example to tell the interviewer about the skills that you used.

AN OUTSTANDING SHARE ANSWER

There are few things better than a good story to lend energy to an interview, and a good yarn presented in the shape of a SHARE answer has the added benefit of driving home a point about your skills. I once asked a retired paratrooper I was interviewing to give me an example of a time when he had to cope with a difficult situation. After a few moments of thought, he began to tell me about a survival program he had undergone as part of his military training:

"After parachuting into the training area, we had the mission of avoiding capture. If we were captured, our mission was to escape. As it turned out, we were 'captured' within hours by the 'enemy'—the training staff. Their 'prison camp guards' interrogated us and put us in their lockup.

"This was supposedly a secure area. It had a dirt floor and crates for us to sleep on. But I found a tunnel under my crate that apparently went under the fence and out of the compound.

"I quickly organized three of us into an escape team and we started to crawl down the tunnel. It opened into a space about three feet deep and wide and continued for about twenty feet, and then it came to a dead end. I told the other two guys to back out and we'd try again. But the hole had been covered up with something heavy. We were stuck.

"One of the guys panicked, screaming to be let out, but I got him to calm down by saying that we had obviously been set up, that the tunnel was a trap, but that it was only an exercise and we'd get out okay. I talked about what we would do later to celebrate surviving the school—we'd go to Hawaii. By the time I got around to describing our beach party, he had settled down. Within an hour or so we were released.

"Now, when I think back on what happened, I feel that it was a profound learning experience for me. I learned that being calm is an important part of problem solving. And I learned that I could exert leadership in helping another person cope with a difficult situation."

I was spellbound by his story. Not only did he answer exactly the question I asked, he used the SHARE format very effectively to illustrate his skill in coping. He described succinctly the difficult situation he and the others had found themselves in; told of the hindrances that arose as they tried to solve problems; explained exactly how he used his skills to overcome those hindrances; told me the results of his actions; and related effectively what he had learned from the experience. Besides conveying to me a sense of what an adventure it was, he showed me that he could be a calming influence on others and that he was willing and able to be a leader.

Of course, a natural storyteller has an advantage over others. Perhaps you don't think of yourself as a first-class yarn spinner, but as you practice putting together your SHARE answers, think of the most dramatic examples you can of each of the skills you want to highlight. Maybe you've overlooked a good example or two. Don't make up tall tales, though, or paint yourself as a super-hero for every situation, or try to make your work history sound like an endless series of adventures. One or two good examples mixed in with more standard fare will be sufficient to heighten the interviewer's interest.

PREPARING YOUR OWN SHARE EXAMPLES

You will now develop SHARE answers which you can use to communicate how you can use your performance skills on the job. First, review the sample SHARE answer on the next page. Next, review the performance skills and questions which might be asked by a behavioral-based interviewer. Then, write out a SHARE example for each of the performance skills that you may want to show-case in the interview. Remember that your skill profile (pages 80–81) can help you identify what you want to emphasize.

This is an especially valuable exercise for three reasons:

1. it gets you into the SHARE answer pattern;

2. it helps you identify and remember the many individual skills that you have developed in your career; and

3. it makes you think through how you will answer similar questions in the interview.

Having in mind examples to discuss will build your confidence and impress the interviewer.

SAMPLE SHARE ANSWER

Skill: Displays Leadership—Communicates thoughts, feelings, and ideas to justify a position; encourages, persuades, or otherwise motivates individuals or groups; challenges existing procedures, policies, or authority responsibly.

Question: "Give me an example of a time when you were able to persuade another person to conform or adapt to work expectations."

Answer:

Situation. "During one project, I was assigned as leader of a team to put together a catalog that one of the other team members had done by himself in the past."

Hindrances. "It quickly became apparent that this team member didn't like having his personal project taken away from him and assigned to the whole team. I knew that he had strong feelings about it, not just because it was his idea originally but because he was concerned that the quality would suffer."

Actions. "I went to his office and asked him straight out to help the other team members maintain the quality standards he had set. I asked him to call a meeting at his convenience to describe the problems he had encountered in past issues and to tell us how he had overcome them. I explained that if the team did a good job, we would probably be assigned many more publications than any one person could handle, so future publications would probably be shepherded by individual team members with the help of all the other members."

Results. "He immediately became enthusiastic about helping to increase the team's responsibilities. He volunteered not only to conduct a brief training session but to consult with each team member as problems arose. Before I left his office, he told me of several improvements he had been thinking about for the next issue and offered to share them with the team at the meeting."

Evaluate. "I felt that, by engaging his sense of being the 'parent' of the catalog, I helped him see how the project had matured and grown too large for any one person to handle; that his experience would be more valuable spread among several publications; and that his good work in the past had put him in line for more responsibility."

PERFORMANCE SKILLS AND SAMPLE QUESTIONS

Adaptability

Shows Resilience: "Tell me about a time when you were able to treat a negative experience as a learning opportunity."

Accommodates Changes: "Give me an example of a time when you first resisted a change at work and then accepted it."

Interpersonal

Participates in Teamwork: "Give me an example of a time when, as a team member, you were cooperative even though you found it difficult."

Displays Leadership: "Can you tell me of a situation in which you were unable to persuade another person to conform to work expectations?"

Manages Conflict: "Describe a time when you had to use courage to express your opinion to your boss, a co-worker, or a work team."

Accepts Differences: "Give me an example of a time when you were able to work effectively with a person from a cultural background that was very different from yours."

Provides Service: "Tell me about an incident in which a customer was so difficult that you just gave up trying to satisfy him or her."

Work Habits

Exhibits Integrity: "Give me an example of a time when you were able to keep a confidence, even when you were tempted to break it."

Manages Oneself: "Tell me about a situation in which you successfully managed yourself without immediate supervision."

Motivates Oneself and Others: "Recount an instance when you showed a sense of urgency in completing a job task. "

Follows Procedures: "Give me an example of a time when you followed policy, even when it made your work more difficult."

WHAT'S NEXT

Now that you have developed a respectable set of SHARE answers about your performance skills, you have several important tasks in front of you. First, you need to develop SHARE answers for your technical skills, those you identified in chapter 5. Each of these skills is described in general terms, because there are so many different technical skills any reader could have. Choose the general categories that apply to you, and develop SHARE examples to illustrate your particular job skills.

You may have noticed that most of the questions for which you composed SHARE answers in this chapter were positive questions. However, I included some negative queries along with them to remind you that the behavioral-based interviewer will ask you for some negative examples as well. For example, the question under "Accepts Differences" was "Give me an example of a time when you were able to work effectively with a person from a cultural background that was very different from yours." After you answer this question in the interview, the behavioral-based interviewer may follow up with a negative question: "Now tell me about a time when you were not so successful in working with someone from another culture."

To be doubly prepared for a behavioral-based interview, formulate several negative SHARE examples to go with your positives. But try to frame them in a more positive light. Wrap up your answer by explaining how you learned from the experience, or tell the interviewer how you were able to solve the problem by using other competencies or technical skills.

WHEN THE GOING GETS ROUGH

It's easy enough to answer straightforward questions about your skills if you're prepared and have practiced using the skill-benefit and SHARE formats aloud. But how do you respond when the questions get personal, pointed, embarrassing, invasive, hostile, or even illegal? As you will see in the next chapter, the SHARE technique can be adapted to fit almost any situation, even the tough ones. You will learn how to answer these questions candidly and accurately while doing as little damage as possible to your interview ratings.

CHAPTER 8

KILLER QUESTIONS, DYNAMITE ANSWERS

What's the thing you fear most about being interviewed? Being asked a question you can't answer or don't want to answer, right? Sooner or later, someone will ask you that killer question. Incompetent or mediocre interviewers will ask you questions that are illegal, irrelevant, incomprehensible, or intended simply to trip you up. A good interviewer will ask you questions that challenge you, stretch your ability to answer, and let you demonstrate what kinds of skills you have to offer.

Don't worry; for every killer question there's a good, honest answer. As long as you're prepared to answer in a way that will keep you in the running as a candidate, you don't have to fear killer questions. Some you can even use to your advantage. If you can give a dynamite answer, you can earn extra points from the interviewer.

In this chapter you will learn how to use the techniques you've learned so far to respond to these questions. You can adapt your skill-benefit statements to make your point quickly, or use the SHARE answer format when you need to document exactly what you did. Regardless of which approach you take, remember that your objective is to use every question, no matter how adverse, as an opportunity to demonstrate what you can do on the job.

IN THIS CORNER, THE KILLER...

There are several kinds of killer questions. The following list shows the range— from the sublime to the ridiculous.

Killer Questions

- **Illegal questions.** Questions relating to a candidate's gender, race, color, national origin, religion, age, or disabilities are usually illegal. Women probably get asked the most illegal questions—those about children. "How will you take care of your children when they are sick?" is out of line; it assumes that the mother will have problems with child care and may even suggest that she should be home caring for the kids. Whether asked of women or men, questions about family planning and home responsibilities are also illegal but not uncommon. There are ways to deal with these questions.

- **Pet-theory questions.** Managers develop their own pet theories about success. Some are based on valid experience and observation, such as the way successful performers usually behave. Some interviewers, however, cannot get past certain irrational notions, such as the theory that graduates of a particular university (the interviewer's) are prone to success, or that athletes make the best salespersons. It's hard to overcome a pet theory—you can't change your alma mater or become a star athlete on a moment's notice—but with a little preparation, you can compensate by drawing attention to your real qualifications.

- **Hot-topic questions.** A lot of people have parts of their history that they'd rather no one knew about—drug or alcohol abuse, a nasty divorce, cancer, prison time. Even though you may have triumphed over some earlier problem, naturally you fear that the topic might arise; some sensitive facts may be public information. You can't rewrite your life, but you can build a plan to deal with the topic if it emerges.

- **"Gotcha" questions.** When the interviewer tries to lead you into an answer by phrasing her question, "Don't you think that . . ." you should be concerned that whatever you say will be wrong. In the belief that there's something negative about you that needs to be either confirmed or disproven, she's probably trying to get you to admit to a problem. But you can confound the interviewer's expectations and advance your case with a good answer.

- **Questions out of your experience.** If you're a recent college graduate, you may have very little work experience to draw on to answer questions, or you may be asked about technical skills that are not yet in your repertoire. You can recognize these questions because you don't need time to think of an answer—you know you don't have one. But you can compensate by selecting a part of your background that can be linked to the question. Naturally, don't take this so far that you seem to be evading the question.

- **Double-trouble questions.** This kind of question is actually very clever: the interviewer poses a question which, when answered, will provide negative information about you. A behavioral-based interviewer might ask, "When have you found it necessary to put your work over your family?" Another version is phrased as a hypothetical question: "What would you do if you suspected that your best friend at work was using sick days to add to vacation time?" You can answer these questions honestly yet advantageously if you stay alert.

- **Questions for negative information.** These questions, typical of those you might expect from a well-trained behavioral-based interviewer, are phrased as a reverse of information that you have already given. For example, "Describe a time when you put in extra effort to get a job done on time" might be followed by "Now, describe a time when you didn't work as hard as you should have."

COACH'S TIP

In a fencing class, you quickly learn the importance of the words "on guard." It means to be ready for whatever may come your way. Many candidates miss out on good opportunities by mishandling a single question. You have to be prepared to defend yourself the whole time you are engaged with the interviewer. Otherwise, you may achieve a near-perfect performance with one fatal mistake.

....AND OVER HERE, KID DYNAMITE

You can handle killer questions using any of the following techniques. Each is aimed at a particular kind of question, but the best way to use them is to find ways to combine them. Adapt your skill-benefit statements and SHARE examples as needed to respond to each question.

On the following pages you will find techniques for giving good answers to difficult questions. They are:

- Highlight a compensating strength
- Present diverse benefits
- Apply damage control
- Show learning from mistakes
- Disagree tactfully
- Admit that you are not perfect

Once you understand the technique, select a question that relates to you and use the form to answer it.

YEAH-BUT

It seems you are asking me to be a chameleon, changing my colors based on the question I am asked. I prefer to give my true answer, regardless of who asks it. I am who I am.

COACH'S COMEBACK

I admire your integrity. But I am not asking you to be dishonest. I am showing you how to phrase your answers to protect yourself from an interviewer who is subjective, biased, and manipulative. Rather than a chameleon, I want you to be a butterfly. You went through a phase when you were less than attractive, but now you are transformed, a beautiful, admirable creature who can flit expertly on the breeze.

HIGHLIGHT A COMPENSATING STRENGTH

When the interviewer asks you to talk about one of your weak points, answer honestly, and follow through by highlighting a strength that compensates for the weakness. Show that you can recognize your own failings and learn from them. Give an example of a situation in which you made a mistake but used another skill to accomplish the same thing, limit the damage, or even improve the outcome. If you acknowledge that you're less than a top-notch organizer and planner, emphasize that you compensate for it with high skills in following policy and procedures.

Applications

- Questions for negative information
- Questions out of your experience

Sample Questions

Gut-feel: What is your weak point?

Trait: Which of the following traits is most like you? Are you more selfish, more hard-headed, or more disorganized?

Conversational: Often a core value and a weakness go hand in hand. How do you feel that your weakness relates to a core value?

Behavioral-based: Give me an example of a time when your biggest weakness at work kept you from reaching an important objective.

Answer Guide

1. *State your area for improvement.*
One of the characteristics I need to improve is _____.

2. *Highlight a strength that will compensate for the weakness.*
As I improve in this area, I try to use my skill in _____
_____ to help me avoid making any big mistakes.

3. *Describe a past event that shows how you successfully used the strength to compensate for your weakness.*
For example, _____
_____.

I am especially proud of the way that I was able to _____
_____
_____.

4. *Describe another past event that shows your learning.*
I remember a similar situation involving _____
_____.

My actions were constrained in this situation because _____
_____.

What I did was to _____
_____.

This resulted in _____
_____.

I learned _____
_____.

This was shown later when I _____
_____
_____.

PRESENT DIVERSE BENEFITS

Some interviewers look for a knockout factor, the one thing about you that they think disqualifies you. Often it's a pet theory: "Women with children can't work late." Sometimes it's a gut feeling: "Too much like that last guy I hired." Deal with these hidden knockout factors by emphasizing so many different skills that you override them. Answer the question with a skill-benefit statement; then add another skill-benefit statement related to the question, and perhaps another.

Applications

- Double-trouble questions
- "Gotcha" questions
- Pet-theory questions

Sample Questions

Gut-feel: "A little voice inside my head tells me that you have a problem with giving 100 percent to the job. Am I right?"

Trait: "Sooner or later we're all a little lazy. To what extent are you a 'lazy' person?"

Conversational: "Do you have a problem with working late in the evenings?"

Behavioral-based: "Give me an example of a time when you didn't work as hard as you could have."

Answer Guide

1. *Test your understanding by stating your interpretation of what the interviewer really wants to know.*

Let me be sure I understand what you need to know. I think that your question relates to _____

_____

_____.

Am I right?

Okay, let me give you some indications of _____

_____

_____

by describing some of the things I have done.

2. *Make a skill-benefit statement.* _____

_____

_____.

3. *Make another skill-benefit statement.* _____

_____

_____.

4. *Ask whether you have given enough information on your skill.*

Can I elaborate on any of these points?

_____

_____.

APPLY DAMAGE CONTROL

Even if you are a very skilled individual and highly qualified for the job, you may have a serious problem or character-related shortcoming in your past—bankruptcy, termination for cause, DWI conviction—that you have overcome and would rather not dwell on. However, the interviewer may have documented evidence of it and may be very direct about wanting to discuss it with you. You can reduce the impact by showing, with humility, how you have learned from the experience. If the negative was the result of a character defect, show that you have changed for the better; give examples of times when you demonstrated this. State that you are committed never to make that mistake again. In general, don't volunteer information about your past difficulties, but don't try to hide it if you are asked directly about it.

Application

- Hot-topic questions

Sample Questions

Gut-feel: "What do you consider the biggest screw-up in your life?"

Trait: "How has your self-esteem been set back by a negative experience?"

Conversational: "What would you like to change about your past?"

Behavioral-based: "Tell me about a time at work when you disappointed yourself by not following your principles."

Answer Guide

1. *Reflect humility.*
This period of my life had some things about it that I'm not very proud of. At that time I had a problem with _____

_____

_____

_____.

2. *Briefly describe a past event that shows what you learned from your negative experience.*
Since then I have learned how to _____

_____

_____.

3. *State your commitment to battle the thing that caused the negative.*
I remain committed to _____

_____

_____.

4. *Show your optimism about your future.*
And I feel a great deal of optimism about the future. This is because I

_____

_____

_____.

SHOW LEARNING FROM MISTAKES

An interviewer may, with or without evidence, ask you to identify and discuss a mistake you made on the job. A skilled interviewer will ask for examples of times when you were not effective in using a skill. You can turn this question to your advantage by telling what went wrong and what you learned from it. Support your answer with an example of a time when you used what you learned from the experience. Be specific; show that you can identify mistakes and convert them to principles that you can apply in other situations.

Application

- Questions for negative information

Sample Questions

Gut-feel: "I believe in people who are tough. Tell me, in what ways have you been too easy on people?"

Trait: "It seems to me that you are so sensitive that you may overreact to negative comments from customers. Is this true?"

Conversational: "How do you feel about interpersonal conflict at work?"

Behavioral-based: "Describe a time when you were not effective in managing conflict at work."

Answer Guide

1. *Describe how you recognized the mistake, hopefully before others saw it.*

When dealing with _____, I tend to focus on being direct and reasonable.

2. *Describe reasonable actions you took or planned to take.*

In this situation, I was reasonable in what I did because _____ _____.

3. *Describe what you learned from the experience.*

In this situation, I learned to _____ _____.

4. *Describe another past event that shows your learning.*

I remember a similar situation involving _____ _____.

My actions were constrained in this situation because _____ _____.

What I did was to _____ _____.

This resulted in _____ _____.

I learned _____ _____.

This was shown later when I _____ _____.

5. *State your conclusion about yourself.*

My conclusion is that I am _____ _____ _____.

DISAGREE TACTFULLY

The interviewer may have certain negative assumptions about you, or may draw incorrect negative conclusions from one of your answers: "I understand that the position you held in your last organization was considered a low-skill job," or "From what you've just told me, there are times you're not as disciplined as you should be." You can counter these false conclusions by tactfully disagreeing with the interviewer's interpretation: "I can see how you might draw that conclusion, but I have to disagree. I may seem unconcerned with minor points, but I'm very disciplined on the important parts of my job. For example, in the situation I just described...."

Applications

- Illegal questions
- Double-trouble questions
- "Gotcha" questions
- Pet-theory questions

Sample Questions

Gut-feel: "People from your type of background typically don't do well in leadership positions in our organization. Why should I give you a chance?"

Trait: "What is your leadership style? Would people say that you are too participative to make a quick decision?"

Conversational: "Wouldn't you agree that most leaders fail because of a low IQ?"

Behavioral-based: "Give me an example of a time when you were disappointed with your ability to lead."

Answer Guide

1. *Recognize the interviewer's reasoning by restating key parts of the question.*
I can see the reasoning behind your question. You are saying that

_____

_____

_____.

2. *Say that you can't agree with all of the interviewer's reasoning.*
On the other hand, this is a very complex topic and I can't agree that

_____

_____

_____.

3. *Give an example from your past to make your point.*
For example, when I worked at _____ I dealt with a situation
in which _____.
I was hindered by _____

_____.

The actions I took were _____

_____.

The result was _____

_____.

I would evaluate the results by saying that _____

_____.

4. *State your conclusion about yourself.*
My conclusion is that I am _____

_____

_____.

DILUTE THE NEGATIVE

Remember that the interview is not a career-counseling session. Although it's best to admit mistakes and acknowledge shortcomings, the interviewer will focus on what is wrong with you if you spend too much time dwelling on your faults. Admit that you're not perfect, then move on quickly to your assets. Accentuate the positive by following the 5/55 rule: admit your negative in 5 seconds, then spend the next 55 seconds talking about your more positive attributes. "Yes, I have to admit that I'm sometimes impatient with people. But I think in the long run this works to the customer's benefit, because I'm impatient with co-workers who don't follow customer-oriented procedures. When I worked at XYZ, I had to tell one co-worker that. . . ."

Application

- Questions for negative information

Sample Questions

Gut-feel: "Everybody I contacted about you says that you're weak when it comes to attention to detail. How do you respond to that?"

Trait: "Are you the type of person who will make a decision, even if you have to break a policy involving safety?"

Conversational: "How do you feel about following policy and procedures that actually slow down your work?"

Behavioral-based: "When have you not followed a procedure that you should have followed?"

Answer Guide

1. *Briefly recognize the negative.*

There could be a pretty negative outcome if I _____

_____

_____.

2. *Describe at greater length a positive example that honestly minimizes the negative.*

On the other hand, I know that _____

_____

_____.

Let me give an example that relates to this issue. The situation involved _____

_____.

I was hindered by _____

_____.

The actions I took were _____

_____.

The result was _____

_____.

I would evaluate the results by saying that _____

_____.

3. *State your conclusion about yourself.*

My conclusion is that I am _____

_____

_____.

DISTINGUISH BETWEEN TRAITS AND BEHAVIOR ===

There's a big difference between a negative trait and negative behavior. You may tend to be too extroverted, too suspicious, too impatient—but you can control what you say and do. When an interviewer accurately discerns that you have a negative trait, agree: "Yes, you're right, I have a tendency to avoid situations in which there's likely to be some conflict." Then point out that you have the tendency under control and that it does not determine what you actually do. You can further enhance your case by describing how you use other skills productively to compensate. "Not only did I learn to stay calm when dealing with angry co-workers, but I got pretty good at using my planning and communication skills to avoid the misunderstandings. Shortly after the incident I just described, I realized that we weren't giving our people enough advance warning about. . . ."

Applications

- Questions for negative information
- Double-trouble questions
- "Gotcha" questions
- Pet-theory questions

Sample Questions

Gut-feel: "You don't seem to be very flexible. How do you feel about working in a place where everything is topsy-turvy?"

Trait: "You don't appear to be willing to change in order to adapt to your job. To what extent is this true?"

Conversational: "How do you feel when dealing with an uncomfortable level of change at work?"

Behavioral-based: "Tell me about a time when you were not successful in adapting to change."

Answer Guide

1. *Acknowledge that you have a slightly negative trait.*

I have to agree with you that I am not very _____

_____.

2. *Explain how you keep the negative under control.*

I use my understanding of this tendency to help me _____

_____.

3. *Give an example of an incident in which you overcame your negative trait.*

For example, I used my self-discipline to control my tendency to be

_____ when I dealt with a situation involving _____

_____.

I was hindered by _____

_____.

The actions I took were _____

_____.

The result was _____

_____.

I would evaluate the results by saying that _____

_____.

4. *State a conclusion involving your self-discipline.*

My conclusion is that I am _____

_____

_____.

ADMIT THAT YOU ARE NOT PERFECT

To acknowledge imperfection is simply to be realistic. It shows the interviewer that you have a firm grasp of reality, that you know you're human and fallible. Do not, of course, volunteer your shortcomings in response to every question. Keep in mind that you want to be competitive. But when asked about your negatives, describe yourself as a work in progress and state that you enjoy the process of continuous self-improvement.

Application

- Questions for negative information

Sample Questions

Gut-feel: "It sounds like you solve problems by taking the day off. Why can't you tackle things head on?"

Trait: "What is the biggest flaw in your personality when you get your feelings hurt?"

Conversational: "What is the number one principle that you follow when you are having a problem with job stress?"

Behavioral-based: "Tell me about a time when you were not successful in coping with a pressure situation."

Answer Guide

1. *Acknowledge that you are not perfect.*
I have to admit that I am not perfect. One of my areas for personal
growth involves _____

_____.

I am committed to continuous self-improvement. When I discover an
area where I need personal growth, or where I have a problem with
one of my skills, I develop a plan to use one of my strengths to help
me improve.

2. *Give an example that shows that you are constantly learning.*
For example, in a situation involving _____

_____, I faced the problem of

_____

_____.

I was hindered by _____

_____.

The actions I took were _____

_____.

The result was _____

_____.

I would evaluate the results by saying that _____

_____.

My conclusion is that I am _____

_____.

RESPONDING TO AN ILLEGAL QUESTION

Odds are that if you are interviewed more than a few times you will be asked at least one illegal question. When it happens, you need to be ready for it and respond in a way that maximizes your chances of getting the job, or at least minimizes the damage. Your first impulse may range from challenging the interviewer directly to breaking off the interview and calling a lawyer. Of course you have the right, but you shouldn't take such a move lightly. Your anger may have faded, you may even have found a better job, long before the process has run its course. It's emotionally draining and expensive, it distracts you from your job search, and the results may disappoint you. Only one person is assured of employment: your lawyer.

You can respond to an illegal question in many different ways; each entails a different combination of risk and opportunity. Refusing to answer is the riskiest tactic; although it's not as confrontational as reacting with overt anger or taking the organization to court, it can put a stop to unfair questioning. However, I know of few candidates who have advanced in the screening process by refusing to answer illegal questions.

WHEN THEY'VE GOT YOU DEAD TO RIGHTS

Sometimes you have to expect the interviewer to ask you point blank about one of your negatives:

"Why were you fired?"

When this happens, there's nothing for it but to own up as smoothly as possible and quickly shift attention to the more positive aspects of it.

1. *Preface your answer by explaining the circumstances.*
Sometimes you just get into a complex situation with difficult personalities . . .

2. *Very briefly and succinctly, tell the truth.*
   . . . and this was one of those times. Yes, I was fired.

3. *At some length, go on to explain what you learned from the experience.*
However, by watching this person's effect on those around him, I did learn to be more alert to the political environment at work.

4. *Continue at length to convert the experience to a benefit: How can your experience be of benefit to the organization in your new job?*
I expect to use this experience to help create an atmosphere of respect and civility in my new place of work.

THE JOY OF SKILLFUL EVASION

Some candidates, when asked blatantly illegal questions, manage to answer with humor or divert the interviewer's attention from the topic. If you're good at thinking on your feet, you may be tempted to do likewise, and you may be successful in deflecting the bias in the question. But be warned: some interviewers may consider you sarcastic or aggressive.

Q: "Mrs. Jones, tell me about your family."

A: "My mother takes care of our two children and my husband has had a vasectomy."

Q: "How are you going to feel when you make sales calls on white customers?"

A: "I'll feel proud of the quality product line I represent."

Q: "Do you regard yourself as being a person of color?"

A: "Yes. I qualify as an Equal Employment Opportunity statistic, in case you have an audit."

Q: "Do you go to church on Sunday?"

A: "It depends on how much I have to do at work."

Q: "Were your parents immigrants?"

A: "My father told me that everyone who's not an American Indian is an immigrant."

Q: "How old are you?"

A: "I'm old enough to appreciate the importance of doing a good day's work every day."

Q: "Do you have any health problems?"

A: "Yes. I'm a workaholic."

COACH'S TIP

Practice, Practice, Practice! You cannot memorize your answers to killer questions and expect to deliver them credibly. You must practice your answers—aloud! If you can arrange it, have someone ask you these sample killer questions and then critique the way you dealt with them.

Suppose the interviewer says to you, a Japanese-American, "Some of our older guys down in Shipping are World War II veterans. They may give you a hard time. Do you think you can keep that from getting under your skin?"

Although the insulting nature of the question makes you want to explode, you control your anger. Looking directly at the interviewer, you calmly say, "I don't believe I care to answer that question." This response indicates that such a situation would not be acceptable to you; furthermore, it puts the interviewer on notice that you may consider taking legal action if you get a negative evaluation. However, the risk you take is that the interviewer may search hard for a legitimate reason to disqualify you.

Another way to respond to illegal questions is to answer directly, then continue by addressing the interviewer's concerns and giving positive information about your skills. For example, the interviewer asks you, a female candidate, "How do you feel about latchkey kids?" You respond directly:

"I agree that young children need someone at home for them all the time. But my kids are older, and they've learned how to take care of themselves. They know they can contact me or their father in case of emergency. They have become more responsible and self-reliant, and by being dedicated to my work, I'm giving them a good role model."

This answer deals with the concern of the interviewer, whether it is legal or illegal. Second, it lets you promote one of your performance skills—your dedication to your work. You could extend this answer by giving a SHARE example of a time when you successfully completed a crucial project while handling a minor domestic crisis. You could talk about other, related skills that you brought to the job, such as your ability to handle crises calmly and efficiently.

THE WINNER, BY A DECISION . . .

Dealing with negative information is tricky. The untrained interviewer tends to be suspicious of positive information—since it's obviously to your advantage to offer it—and thus tends to overreact to negative information, on the assumption that it is more accurate. A skilled interviewer, on the other hand, uses negative information to judge your grasp of reality and your willingness to learn and improve. With a typical interviewer, therefore, it may be in your best interest to minimize negative information. With a skilled interviewer, you can be more open.

Now that you've seen a few samples of how tough the questions can be, you may feel discouraged about getting out of an interview alive. So much information, so much to remember—by now you may have overloaded your circuits and tripped a breaker. But don't worry; if you've identified the negatives you're likely to be asked about and planned just a few responses, you're well equipped to answer a wide variety of other questions. You may find yourself using responses you've framed for these killer questions to answer positive questions as well. Once prepared, trust yourself.

PART THREE

PREPARE
TO
PROMOTE
YOURSELF

During a recent economic downturn I saw a picture of an unemployed stock broker, on Wall Street, wearing a huge sandwich sign: "Have M.B.A. Will work long hours." People were staring with amazement; if he wasn't getting job offers, at least he was getting attention. I thought to myself, There has to be a better way—a way he could get interviews and still keep his dignity.

A few weeks later, I was greeting customers in our booth at a human resources convention. A man approached the booth wearing an electronic bow tie. "Hire Me," it flashed. My immediate reaction was, "No way!" His effort was bold, but lacking in taste and character—in a word, unprofessional.

It was a gut reaction, I confess. I'm a person who usually avoids making snap judgments; yet my immediate reaction was unfavorable. Why go out of your way to bias a potential employer against you? There's a big difference between getting attention and getting a positive reaction. Even if the initial impression is favorable, it is probably a reaction to the candidate's directness rather than his qualifications.

Successful self-promotion goes well beyond simply getting attention or getting an interview; it means getting the deck stacked in your favor up front. People who are successful at promoting themselves are rarely seen as self-promoters. Instead, they seem businesslike, good at communicating what they can do. Typically, they have

- a career story that is interesting to an interviewer;
- a résumé that emphasizes their skills;
- a good telephone presence; and
- an in-house advocate.

Not only are these communication tools crucial in getting interviews, they can work for you even more powerfully during the interview and after. They can create a positive bias—a momentum—that carries through in your favor long after your initial contact.

The next four chapters will show you how to build that favorable bias and get the momentum going in your favor. In chapter 9 you will see that a good career story can be built on the same elements as a good movie script or a heroic legend. Chapter 10 tells you how to use written materials, especially your résumé, to influence the way you are seen and interviewed. Chapter 11 gives you tips on how to use the telephone effectively, both for making initial contact and for a telephone interview. And chapter 12 provides insight into getting a person inside the organization to present your case when you aren't there.

CHAPTER 9

MAKE YOUR CAREER STORY MAGIC

"Pick a point in your life that reflects the real beginning of your work life. Then trace it to the present, giving me a summary of your education and work experiences."

It's not that tough a question. It's not personal, not prejudicial, not a "gotcha" question. It invites you to choose your starting point, to describe your education and jobs in your own terms, and to emphasize whatever skills you have that are relevant to the job you are interviewing for.

Then why are some responses to this career-story question as compelling as a Shakespearean drama, while others come across as "just the facts, ma'am"?

In my years of taking notes during interviews, I've become very good at recording my thoughts about the organization, grammar, and thoroughness of candidates' responses to this start-up work-history question. Yet my notes couldn't tell me exactly why some candidates' careers sounded exciting and magical while others, though equally impressive on the surface, seemed to hold less interest.

My curiosity about this set me thinking, and I believe I've come up with a clue. In retrospect, the interesting careers seemed like a good action-adventure movie or an exciting journey. Candidates with "magical" careers gave their stories extra sparkle. Perhaps intuitively, they structured their responses the way a good story teller would. They did more than just recite names, dates, skills, duties, and responsibilities; they conveyed their excitement and joy at having found a purpose, struggled to overcome obstacles, and used their abilities to accomplish the mission.

THE VALUE OF ADVERSITY

I think it's the struggle that makes the story so compelling. I once interviewed about fifty people in one company. Most of them had a sense of purpose in their careers and were willing to do battle on the issues they felt were important. Long before I was finished, I began to realize that many of their career histories shared certain themes: a childhood disrupted by poverty or alcohol, guidance in developing a rock-solid work ethic, and a strong sense of right and wrong.

This is not to say that a dysfunctional family is a prerequisite for a good career story. Early interests and experiences in a positive childhood are just as influential. The driving factor seems to be the struggle to fulfill a mission—especially a mission conceived early in life. For example, many airline pilots had a passion for aviation since childhood; people in creative professions often experienced solitude; law enforcement officers typically spent formative years in sports and physical activities; and attorneys were often encouraged to develop their reading and writing skills.

THE START-UP QUESTION

First, let's look at what you can expect as the interview begins. An experienced interviewer usually starts off with pleasantries intended to build rapport, then progresses smoothly into the information-gathering phase of the interview, in which the questions relate directly to your skills and qualifications. To smooth the transition, the interviewer will begin the information-gathering phase with what can be termed "start-up" questions.

There are two basic kinds of start-up questions: the "descriptive" question and the "background" question. The interviewer using a descriptive question asks one or more questions to help you quickly describe who you are and what you know about the employer. These questions can be perfectly reasonable

SAMPLE RESPONSE TO A DESCRIPTIVE QUESTION

Although they cover a wide range of potential topics, standard descriptive questions are fairly predictable. Handling them successfully can smooth your way to success in the remainder of the interview.

Question: "Why are you looking for a new job?"

Answer: *Restating key words in the question*
I am looking for a new job . . .

Your direct answer to the question
. . . mainly to test the waters and see if I can find opportunities to use more of my skills. Our firm is in a state of constant turmoil because of restructuring and changes in our product line. I feel that your company is in a better competitive position, and I want to see if I can fit into your growth plans.

Trait, value, or skill
I've always believed in upgrading my skills to keep up with the needs of the organization. Right now I've got training and experience with twelve different software packages for business applications. I'm also taking continuing education classes on business planning software that links financial resources to individual projects . . .

Benefit to the employer
. . . so I'll have the necessary skills ready to use on my first day at work.

---

ways to quickly find out who you are, or they can be questions that intimidate or embarrass you. You should be prepared to respond to any of them.

The Descriptive Question

Your response to a descriptive question can usually follow a basic series of steps:

- Restate the key words in the question, giving you time to think.
- Give a direct answer to the question.
- Mention one of your strong traits, values, or skills.
- Conclude with a benefit to the employer.

The sample response above shows a descriptive question and a way to respond to it.

Here are some other standard descriptive questions that might catch you off guard; select four or five and prepare direct answers for them.

- Tell me about yourself.
- Why did you leave your last job?

- Why do you want to work for us?
- What do you want out of this job?
- Why should I hire you?
- What are your goals?
- What is your greatest strength?
- What is your main weakness?
- What was your biggest mistake in life?
- What is your biggest regret?
- What is your biggest success in life?
- What do you know about our organization?

The Background Question

The background question, the second kind of start-up question, is the one that lets you put magic into your career story. The interviewer asks you to review your personal, job, or skill history to give the interviewer a general sense of who you are.

Good preparation for this kind of question can earn you a lot of favor in the selection process. Your response should be well organized. Begin with the event the interviewer specifically asks you about, then continue in sequence, stating the time frames aloud. This helps the interviewer keep her notes organized and your presentation coherent. Familiarize yourself with your own history; stumbling or hesitating over details doesn't make you look good.

I think that it is best to respond to a background question by giving a skill-history answer that allows you to talk about your skills, how you learned them, and where you used them. The behavioral-based interviewer wants to know what you can do, what you have done, when you did it, and what your results were. You may be asked to review in sequence the events in your education and working life that were important in developing your skills, competencies, and

---

COACH'S TIP

Instead of emphasizing events in your life, use the start-up question as an opportunity to showcase your skills for the job. The most important thing you should bring out is what your past taught you, not where you were.

REVIEW OF SKILL HISTORY ═══════════════════════════════

Question: Tell me about the aspects of your background that would match the job for which you are being considered.

Job or Education #1: _____   **Time Frame:** _____

While I was there, I achieved _____

and learned how to _____

_____.

Job or Education #2: _____   **Time Frame:** _____

While I was there, I achieved _____

and learned how to _____

_____.

work habits. Other interviewers will be more interested in your personal life or where you worked. In either case your response should reflect where you were, what you achieved, and what skills you learned.

After you've reviewed your job skill history, you're ready to meet the interviewer on her own terms. But you can transcend a mere recitation of events by thinking of your life as an adventure worthy of being portrayed in the movies or as a great legend. Every life, every career has a certain amount of challenge, adversity, and triumph, the essential ingredients of a magical story.

THE STRUCTURE OF A MAGICAL CAREER STORY

Every person has one true career story. Your work history has a context that explains how you came to be where you are today. This "big picture" may not be apparent to you at first. Perhaps you feel you've just stumbled from job to job. But if you reflect, you'll begin to see that an early challenge in your life has had a great influence on the type of work that you enjoy, has energized you to deal with problems, and has provided the satisfaction of mastering at least some of the issues you have had to deal with.

Your one true career story has its challenge, struggle, and resolution. Now your task is to get this story to extend itself—to make it write its own next chapter. You'll achieve this by exploring the structure of the "magical career story," then weaving your own career history—your long-term interests, your productive career struggles, your sense of purpose—around that structure.

YEAH-BUT

It seems a little far out to say that my life is a story with adventure and excitement. My story is pretty dull!

COACH'S COMEBACK

If you feel that your life is dull, then—guess what?—your interviewer may come to the same conclusion. Help your interviewer see the adventure in your career by discovering it yourself. I know that there is some sort of career struggle in your life that is interesting and informative.

We'll look at two different ways to get in touch with the dynamics of your career and develop your career story. The primary approach can be called the "script approach," because it applies the structure used by modern storytellers in movies. The other is the "journey approach," a structure like that of stories from the distant past. You can add this to your primary script if part of your story involves a career disaster such as having your job eliminated.

The Script Approach: Your Career as a Movie

I was first exposed to the "how to" of building a good script in 1982 when Art Bauer suggested that we develop a training video on selection interviewing. The result was *More Than a Gut Feeling*, which became the world's best-selling video on how to conduct a selection interview. In working with the creative team, I was coached on how to develop a good script structure. It involved three basic components—setup, struggle, and resolution.

Think of your career as a Hollywood production. You are writing a one-page treatment of your story that you wish to sell to a studio. You know that the studio representatives are very busy; they have hundreds of other scripts to read and are looking for just about any reason to avoid reading yours. You have five minutes. Here's how you tell your story.[1]

Setup. Your career story begins at a time in your early life when you develop a special interest or have a meaningful educational experience. A challenge that you deal with leads you to discover a special passion, purpose, mission, or commitment that you want to achieve through your career. It may be as basic as earning enough money to pay for the basics in life, or as lofty as a lifelong com-

THEMES FOR YOUR CAREER-STORY SCRIPT

Good to Use	Best to Avoid	Notes
SETUP		
Economic need	Alcoholism	_____
Educational effort	Religion	_____
Learning from travel	Emotional traumas	_____
Valuable guidance	Abuse	_____
STRUGGLE		
Achievement	Sexism	_____
Adapting	Racism	_____
Coping with stress	Health	_____
Changing	Addiction	_____
Teamwork	Withdrawal	_____
Maintaining honesty	Rebellion	_____
Overcoming problems	Use of power	_____
RESOLUTION		
Productive outcomes	Revenge	_____
Personal fulfillment	Disappointment	_____
Earned results	Luck	_____
Commitment	Being conquered	_____
Future vision	Living in the past	_____

mitment to helping others. You use this early experience to establish continuity between who you were then and who you are today as a person at work. (Use 5 percent of your career-story time in the setup.)

Struggle. As you pursue your career destiny, you deal with a series of challenges. Your jobs require both effort and patience. You use mistakes as opportunities to learn. Much of the success that you have along the way can be explained by the guidance you received and the opportunities afforded you. You are humble about the courage, discipline, hard work, and team effort that was required for your success. (Use 90 percent of your time describing the struggle.)

The word "struggle" doesn't have to mean a major conflict requiring a great deal of your energy. It could be an issue or topic that you consider important in understanding your general approach to work, or a recurring challenge that you face. You should, however, avoid topics that can be misinterpreted by an interviewer—family problems, failure in school, disability, sexism, racism.

CAREER-STORY CHECKLIST

Evaluate your career-story script by asking yourself the following questions:

- Does the story show how you used a skill important to the job for which you are being considered?
- Can the story illustrate your integrity and team orientation?
- Does the story show you to be rational and careful in your approach to problems?
- Can the story be used to show your adaptability?
- Can you tell the story without revealing confidential information?
- Can you avoid heavy reference to personal aspects of your life, such as your spouse, children, or finances?
- Can you tell the story without using profanity, stereotypes, or embarrassing information?
- Is the story both true and credible?
- Is the story short enough to be used as an answer?

There are exceptions to this rule; in some cases, only these kinds of struggles can illustrate the commitment you have to your career. But there is a danger that an interviewer's pet theories and prejudices can work against you on these topics. It's usually better to describe your struggle in terms of working with difficult people, achieving with limited resources, or resolving integrity issues. You will find the "Themes for Your Career-Story Script" and the "Career-Story Checklist" on these pages helpful in structuring your career story.

Resolution. There comes a time that is the most fulfilling part of your career. If this point of resolution has already occurred, describe the elements of it that carry into the present. If it is yet to come, describe how it might happen in the job for which you are being considered. Or you could describe as your high point the joy you feel in struggling with the challenges of your work. (Use 5 percent of your story time.)

Keep in mind that, even though we're talking about a movie script, we're not suggesting fiction. You must be honest in every part of your career story. The idea of applying a movie-like treatment is to make your story appealing. Of course, you may choose to emphasize certain themes and avoid others; that is up to you. You might, for instance, wisely choose not to describe your career as a religious commitment, which might make your audience—the interviewer—uncomfortable, but instead talk in terms of adhering to your principles.

Remember that your prospective employer will be most interested in how productive and constructive you can be, not how you triumphed over the evil forces arrayed against you by fomenting a rebellion in your work team or by bringing down an autocrat. Avoid including elements in your story suggesting that you have a bad attitude or personal flaws that are not resolved. Instead, tell how you increased productivity or enhanced the dignity of the people you worked with.

The Journey Approach: Career Disaster and Mythology

Another way to make your career story compelling is to borrow from mythology. Anthropologist Joseph Campbell spent his life documenting myths common to many societies in the form of children's rhymes and adult legends. They are often so embedded in education, rituals, and entertainment that they guide the thinking of people in those cultures. Modern-day storytellers, including candidates who know how to engage the rapt interest of the interviewer in their career reviews, often borrow from the structure of these ancient myths.

Campbell found one story structure that was common to most cultures: the "hero's journey." This journey usually has the following stages:

1. The hero prepares for a journey to his destiny.
2. A disaster requires the hero to take action.
3. The hero battles adversaries and dark forces in himself.
4. The hero is trained for a time by a wise old coach.
5. In a great battle, the hero triumphs over the adversaries and dark forces.
6. The hero becomes a leader recognized for his wisdom.

Notice how these stages are described in words that evoke emotional images: destiny, disaster, dark forces, triumphs, wisdom. These words are different from the words typically used in interviews. You may not feel comfortable using such words to describe the crests and troughs of your career. On the other hand, if you're one of the thousands who have lost their jobs to massive layoffs and downsizing, you may find them quite fitting. Telling your story in these terms may both give you satisfaction and engage the interviewer.

THE HERO'S JOURNEY AND YOUR JOB SEARCH ━━━━

The Hero's Journey	The Search Process
Preparation	Goal setting
Disaster	Unemployment
Dark forces	Problem solving
Wisdom	Coaching
Triumph	Job offer
Position	Good, long-term employment

The script for the *Star Wars* movie trilogy was based partly on Joseph Campbell's hero's journey.[2] Luke Skywalker, not knowing he is destined to become a Jedi knight, loses his family to evil forces out to destroy him. He sets out to avenge the attack but is unsuccessful. The guidance and disciplined training of Yoda prepare him for his battle with Darth Vader. His eventual triumph restores his destiny as a Jedi knight and leader of the forces of good.

With my note pad at my side, I once ran *Star Wars* on my VCR to study the parallels between Luke Skywalker's journey and my own somewhat less picturesque career. Not only did I find that I could link each stage of the mythical hero's journey with events in my own life, I discovered that viewing my career this way gave it an emotional resonance that surprised me, probably because it showed me the depth of my feelings about my work. I found Yoda's advice especially valuable.

Before you think I've lost my mind, try it yourself. Complete the steps of your own hero's journey; see how it makes you feel about your career and yourself.

WEAVING YOUR CAREER STORY

Now that you've outlined your career as both a movie script and a heroic journey, it's but a small step to creating your own career story. You will gain many things by doing this. It will make you aware of mistakes that you can choose not to repeat and skills that you need to acquire and build. It will make your response to the career-history question stronger, more credible, and more emotionally compelling.

First, use the movie-script approach; or review your overall career in terms of the scriptwriter's setup, struggle, and resolution. Then, if you are one of the many whose jobs have been eliminated, add in the hero's journey. I've provided examples. Either, or both, will give you a good framework for reviewing all of your pertinent educational and work experiences with an interviewer.

Here are some general points to follow when using the script approach to construct your career story:

- Begin your career story with an early, meaningful educational or work experience and continue through all the jobs you have held.

- Keep the setup brief. If you cannot identify an important experience that influenced your attitude toward work, you can skip the setup altogether.

- Don't forget that your struggle is a recurring topic that is important to you; it is the issue that you have to deal with in more than one job.

- Tell the truth. Everything you say should be absolutely correct.

- Make your story demonstrate the overall themes, forces, and principles of your work history.

- Avoid topics that might make the interviewer feel uncomfortable.

- Show how you have learned from your experiences.

- If your career story has no resolution, describe the goal that you want to achieve.

When you tell the interviewer your career story, do the following:

- Tell your story in sequence, beginning with early experiences and continuing to the present.

- Be succinct. Stay within the time limits the interviewer gives you.

- Watch the interviewer closely to see whether you are giving the information desired.

- Treat questions as opportunities, not only to give facts, but also to describe such things as skills used and skills learned.

- If negative information comes up, describe what you learned from the experience and give an example of how you used what you learned.

YOUR HEROIC CAREER JOURNEY ════

Steps of the Journey	Notes

PREPARATION
    Developing values
    Education
    Achievements

DISASTER
    Losing your job
    Injury
    Health problem

DARK FORCES
    Dirty politics
    Unfair competition
    Low ethics

WISDOM
    A counselor
    A co-worker or family member
    Reading, video, or class

TRIUMPH
    A positive attitude
    Defeating your enemies
    Passing the interview

POSITION
    Accomplishing the job
    Experiencing respect
    Fulfilling your career destiny

THE SCRIPT APPROACH TO A CAREER STORY: ═══════════
ADVANCING THROUGH EDUCATION

Question: Pick a point in your life that reflects the real beginning of your work life. Then trace it to the present, giving me a summary of your education and work experiences.

Answer:

Setup. "I grew up in a farming community, so I'd have to say my working life began on the farm. Neither of my parents had much education. Frankly, I was embarrassed by their lack of schooling. My self-esteem wasn't the greatest; I had to overcome a feeling of inferiority. But my parents were smarter than I thought. They knew the importance of school, and they encouraged me to get as much education as possible. I learned that I could make my way in the world and hold my own with anybody, and my confidence grew. As you'll see, I've kept on learning as much as I could to keep my skills current."

Struggle. "When I was growing up, I had all of the chores you'd expect of a girl on a farm. However, my first 'real' or off-the-farm job was sacking groceries when I was in high school. I saved enough money to start myself off at Lamar State. I found different kinds of part-time work to pay for my education. At one point I had three part-time jobs.

"I graduated in four years with a degree in sales and marketing. The degree helped me start to work as a sales assistant at Top Tech Products in Houston, which was great, because I wanted to go after my M.B.A. and I liked the University of Houston. In five years I had made regional sales manager, tripled my starting salary, and completed my M.B.A. in marketing. I was a real fiend for work; I probably averaged sixty-five hours a week, and that didn't count my class work.

"I was recruited for my next job by Consolidated Chips, a high-tech manufacturing firm. My combination of direct sales experience and an M.B.A. made me particularly attractive for the job that they had in mind. They needed a vice president of marketing who could not only work with a field sales force but also handle the analytical parts of the job. In the six years I've been in this job, we've doubled our sales force and tripled our gross revenues."

Resolution. "I'm happy with the contribution that I've made at Consolidated. But I don't want to stand still; I want to keep pursuing my long-term objective of constantly learning new skills. That's why I'm here. I'm looking for new opportunities in the operational side of the business."

THE JOURNEY APPROACH TO A CAREER STORY: RECOVERY FROM A REDUCTION IN FORCE

Preparation: "About eighteen months before it happened, I had a pretty good idea that my job was going to be eliminated, so I had time to prepare financially for a job search. I also took a course in solid-state electronics to prepare for a career shift."

Disaster: "When the axe finally fell, I was ready, but the reality of what I had to do was still harsh. Even though I had warned my family that this might happen, it was harder on them than I thought it might be."

Dark forces: "The cutback was actually worse than I expected. Some of the politics got pretty unpleasant about who would go and when. And when the time came, I found that I had a great deal of fear about looking for work in an entirely new field."

Wisdom: "Then I got some really good advice from one of my old profs that helped me get clear of the fear and confusion I was feeling. Basically, it was self-discipline; she told me to work off the anxiety with a daily exercise routine, and to focus on the steps of looking for a job. She said the new skills I had learned would make me a good candidate."

Triumph: "She was right. After about six months of hard exercise and job searching, I was offered a job at Delta Demodulators. It's something I wouldn't have imagined a year earlier, but now I'm working in an industry that has a bright future."

Position: "For the long term, I'll have to work extra hard to prove myself in this new line of work. But that's okay. I enjoy being challenged. I'm meeting my long-term goals, and I'm successfully employed. I consider myself lucky."

YEAH-BUT

This information on the career script and hero's journey doesn't work for me. Tell me a simple way to answer a start-up question.

COACH'S COMEBACK

You're right—these approaches don't work for everyone. That's okay. Just use the skill-history review you saw near the beginning of this chapter.

THE ADVENTURE BEGINS

When you think of your career story in terms of a great adventure, you gain three valuable assets that you can use in the interview:

- you can create and sustain rapport by relating a compelling story that keeps the interviewer wanting to hear more;

- you can present a persuasive case for yourself as a person who can overcome great obstacles on the way to major achievement; and, not least,

- you gain insight into your own capabilities and worth.

Keep these benefits in mind as you read the remaining chapters in this part of the book, which is about preparing the ground for the interview to come. When you communicate in writing with your prospective employers (chapter 10), talk with them on the telephone (chapter 11), and cultivate your advocate in the organization (chapter 12), make your story compelling and persuasive. Never forget that when a good match is made, you and your employer share a two-way relationship; not only do you gain the satisfaction of achievement well rewarded, but the organization benefits by virtue of your skills and accomplishments.

CHAPTER 10

WRITE
YOUR OWN
TICKET

Just before I started this book, my company decided to do a trial run on the effectiveness of a classified ad in our local newspaper for a marketing associate. This person would perform a variety of data-processing, clerical, and telephone duties. We received ninety-nine written responses, only thirty-five of which were written well enough to warrant a telephone interview. Five were good enough to show that the candidate could create complete sentences and spell reasonably well. We interviewed these five, and hired one.

We concluded that the one person we found was worth the effort and expense of screening the other ninety-eight. However, we were shocked to see how poorly most candidates communicated in writing. The fact that most people are so bad at it can work to your advantage. All you have to do is take the time to prepare, or get help in preparing, well-written communications with potential employers.

> ### COACH'S TIP
>
> #### FILL YOUR RÉSUMÉ WITH SKILL-BENEFIT STATEMENTS
>
> Look at the résumé as a way to get advance word to your interviewer concerning the company's advantage in hiring you. You've already seen that, in the interview itself, the skill-benefit statement is a powerful tool for making a vital connection in the interviewer's mind between what you can do and how these skills can benefit the organization. The power of a skill-benefit statement is that it makes the connection explicitly for the interviewer; you don't have to simply hope that the interviewer makes the connection.
>
> Your résumé can accomplish much of this work before you ever arrive for the interview; indeed, it can pave the way for your getting the interview. The difference is that in the résumé you connect your skills explicitly with your past accomplishments. That is, you demonstrate how your skills might benefit the organization by showing how they have been of benefit to other organizations you have worked for. You can also generalize by stating your career goals: You wish to develop and apply your skills in management, or in electronic circuit design, or in medical service planning, toward the goal of increasing sales, or of developing smaller and more powerful instruments, or of improving patient care.

WRITE FOR A POSITIVE REACTION

I have often heard interviewers say, "I need to have the résumé before I do the interview. It helps me get a basic feel for who the candidate is." The evidence is clear that written information can bias an interviewer for or against a candidate. Since many interviewers feel compelled to read as much as they can about you before you arrive, you can take advantage of this fact to help make sure the bias is in your favor.

Some interviewers base their decisions about whom they will see on recommendations by others. Most, however, will read your application, résumé, and letters of recommendation before deciding. Their official goal is to find out whether you meet the minimum qualifications for the job. Secretly, though, and perhaps unconsciously, most are just looking for something

> ### COACH'S TIP
>
> Write your résumé in a way that will structure the interview. The unstructured interviewer will probably use your résumé to guide her questioning.

familiar—where you worked, schools you attended, the name of a reference—that strikes an emotional chord, whether good or bad. They are looking for some way to figure you out before they meet you.

Little things that you write can have big consequences:

- The interviewer reads that your interests include scuba diving, just like the previous employee, who failed in the job. He decides not to interview you.

- In your letter of introduction you refer to your family commitments. The interviewer believes people with family ties make better employees, so you get the interview.

- A letter of reference says that you are a "fine Christian." But the interviewer is agnostic and tosses your résumé.

- Your résumé shows that your long-term goal is to earn a Ph.D. in psychology. The interviewer thinks that you won't be committed to the job. Someone else gets the interview.

See what I mean? You can't always predict what emotional impact your information is going to have on an interviewer. Another interviewer might well have exactly the opposite reaction to each of the above examples. Nevertheless, your best chance lies with giving interviewers written information that is most likely to generate a positive reaction. For this, we can generate a simple list of dos and don'ts.

First, the dos:

- Do emphasize your job and performance skills in your résumé. (Meanwhile, prepare skill-benefit statements that you can use in the interview to illustrate each of these skills.)

- Do show your willingness, in your application, your résumé, and your references, to adapt to a variety of changes and demands in the work environment.

- Do communicate, in your cover letter, your core values: honesty, hard work, and respect for others.

Then, the don'ts:

- Don't list unusual or dangerous hobbies or activities in your résumé or elsewhere. You may be an excellent skydiver, mountain climber, or cave explorer, but to the employer, these make you a risk, not a hero.

- Don't specify your political or religious beliefs. Whether you are Republican, Democrat, Christian, Jew, or Confucian has nothing to do with your qualifications for the job. It may, however, disqualify you in the eyes of some interviewers.

- Don't submit a long list of influential people you know—just include one or two among your references, if appropriate. If you name someone who is famous, at least 20 percent of the public will probably dislike him, perhaps including your interviewer.

- Don't write about your plans for learning new skills. The employer is more interested in what you can do now.

After reading this list, you may be asking the question, "What's left to describe?" Just stick to the basics. Emphasize what you can do to solve the employer's problems and be a good team member. If you can do this clearly, and do it for several high-potential organizations, you'll eventually persuade someone to hire you.

YEAH-BUT

My résumé is already prepared!

COACH'S COMEBACK

I encourage you to coordinate your résumé and correspondence with the specifics you want to communicate in the interview. If you send your résumé before you prepare for the interview, you may miss an opportunity to give a consistent message to the employer.

DON'T LEAVE TIME BOMBS IN YOUR RÉSUMÉ

An acquaintance of mine told me a story about a lesson he learned early in his job-hunting career. One of the jobs he had held as a young man had been to drive an elderly couple around the South in their Cadillac to visit battlefields of the Civil War. Having been raised to respect all races and creeds, he quickly learned to his horror that the man who had hired him was a virulent racist who lost no opportunity to make obscene remarks about every African-American he saw on the street. As quickly as he could, he left that job and soon found a better one.

Years later he applied for a job with a large organization in a southern state and was granted an interview. Not more than a couple of minutes after he sat down, the interviewer, a reserved Southern-gentleman type, held up his résumé and asked, "What do you mean by this job description: 'Chauffeured aged bigot from one end of Dixieland to the other'?"

Rattled, my friend managed to maintain his composure long enough to consider his error. Finally he offered a noncommittal explanation that he and his former employer had disagreed on certain philosophical matters and that he was not fired but left on principle. He was eventually hired, but never learned whether, or how hard, he had stepped on the interviewer's toes.

STRUCTURE YOUR RÉSUMÉ

Most interviewers don't use a structured interview form. Instead, they "go with their gut," using first impressions, intuitions, and pet theories to make hiring decisions. This gives you an opening: if the interviewer has no structure in mind, you can impose your own.

A well-developed structured interview is based on job requirements. Motivated by the need for particular kinds of information on job and performance skills, the interviewer asks you the same or similar questions as she does all other candidates. When you prepare for a standardized interview like this, you can control the answers you give—but not the questions you are asked.

An unstructured interview, however, is a different animal. Not only can you control your answers, you can also influence the questions. The key is your résumé.

Here's how a typical unstructured interviewer gets ready to meet you. A few minutes before your interview is to begin, he picks up a folder containing your correspondence, application, and résumé. He skims through the file,

> ## COACH'S TIP
>
> ### DESIGN YOUR RÉSUMÉ FOR COMPUTER SORTING
>
> Many large organizations use a scanner to input your résumé into computer files and sort your information for recruiting. The system scans for key words associated with such things as job titles, technical skills, education, cities where you were employed, and prior employers. In order to make sure that your résumé is screened in by a recruiter, include as many descriptive terms as possible about your skills and career. Also, be sure that your résumé is typewritten in a readable font.

forms a general impression of how well you would fit the job, and formulates a loose plan on what to cover in the interview. Perhaps on your application or résumé he will scribble some notes or write out a few questions to ask you.

This is where the design of your résumé comes into play. If you've structured it so that the interviewer can see all your job skills in a quick scan, his notes and questions will be influenced by what he sees. Programmers have slyly used this approach for years; a sharp engineer lists at the top of her résumé the programs in which she has expertise.

If you wish, you might also steer the interviewer to ask you about either "hard skills" like programming or "soft skills" such as teamwork, depending on where you think your strengths lie. If you consider creativity to be your main skill, front-load your résumé with clear examples of your most creative work.

Most résumés I see are of little help in influencing the questions in an unstructured interview. They describe where the candidate worked, but not what she did. Even if they mention accomplishments, they rarely present an integrated picture of what the applicant can do in the job. Their layout doesn't guide the interviewer to ask the questions that would be most favorable for the candidate.

The Chronological Résumé

You are probably most familiar with, and perhaps even have used in your current résumé, the standard format in which the jobs are listed in chronological order, with the most recent at the top of the page. The problem with this

CHRONOLOGICAL RÉSUMÉ

Joan Durban
12 Poplar Ave.
Hope, Arkansas

Experience

1992–present Assistant to the Chief Engineer, Homes, Inc., Hope, Arkansas, a small rural low-income housing development firm with state-funded business of $1,300,000 annually. Supervised foundation design team of 3 engineers in implementation of CAD software. Salary $3,045/mo.

1989–1992 Planner, Engineering Division, City of Little Rock, Arkansas. Responsible for researching availability of new technologies for cutting costs of maintaining, repairing, upgrading, and expanding municipal sewer system. Salary $2,450/mo.

1985–1989 Architectural Planner I, Department of Recreation, City of Avalon, New Jersey. Assisted in conversion of military facilities to playgrounds in low-income neighborhoods. Salary $1,800/mo.

Education Columbia School of Architecture, M.S. Architectural Engineering, 1985. Colorado School of Mines, B.S. Civil Engineering, 1982.

arrangement is that it tells the interviewer little, at first glance, about the skills you used on the job or your accomplishments in that position. It also puts the spotlight on a position that you may have just lost or are preparing to leave under unpleasant circumstances.

Since your résumé is one of the first formal documents from which the interviewer may form an impression of your qualifications, you should take steps to emphasize those qualifications. The standard format does little to tell your potential employer exactly what tasks you performed or what you accomplished at your past jobs.

Nevertheless, this basic format can be useful if you take steps to highlight your accomplishments. Next, you will see two variations that can significantly improve your chances of steering the interview in a direction favorable to you.

The Skill-Based Chronological Résumé

The skill-based résumé is more straightforward in its promotion of the candidate's capabilities. An interviewer scanning this kind of résumé fifteen minutes before meeting the candidate would quickly gain an impression of a person ready to discuss her most recent achievements. He would be less likely to wonder or ask about the circumstances under which she is leaving her current position. This immediately puts a positive spin on what is not necessarily a positive situation.

In the example shown, the candidate has broken out several short paragraphs to show what actions she took and what the results were. Note that, after

SKILL-BASED CHRONOLOGICAL RÉSUMÉ

Joan Durban
12 Poplar Ave.
Hope, Arkansas

Career goal	A position in senior management of a regional architectural firm.
Education	Columbia School of Architecture, M.S. Architectural Engineering, 1985. Colorado School of Mines, B.S. Civil Engineering, 1982.
Experience	
1992–present	**Assistant to the Chief Engineer, Homes, Inc., Hope, Arkansas,** a small rural low-income housing development firm with state-funded business of $1,300,000 annually. Directly supervised foundation planning team of 3 engineers. Accomplishments:

> **Developed** a design strategy that increased by 225 percent the number of concrete slabs that could be poured using the standard set of forms, thereby reducing project overhead by 26 percent.
>
> **Initiated** the use of state-of-the-art CAD software into the firm's planning unit, allowing a 66 percent reduction in time required to develop new floor plans, reducing cost by an additional 11 percent.

generally outlining her area of responsibility in each position, Joan uses action words such as "developed," "researched," and "trained" to describe specifically what she has accomplished in her current job. Such words help the reader (probably the interviewer) understand clearly the candidate's duties, actions, and achievements.

Note also that the candidate begins with a clear statement of her career objective, states her accomplishments numerically wherever possible, and does not mention salary. She also puts her educational achievements up front; if they were less impressive, she might be wise to leave them to the end.

	Researched and proposed purchase of new computer and networking hardware to allow maximum benefit of new CAD software.
	Trained staff of 7 engineers in the use of new CAD software and hardware.
1989–1992	**Planner, Engineering Division, City of Little Rock, Arkansas.** Responsible for researching availability of new technologies for cutting costs of maintaining, repairing, upgrading, and expanding municipal sewer system.
	Saved over $680,000 in public funds by revising outdated material specifications and by recommending use of new materials and trenching technologies.
	Improved the city's procedures for monitoring equipment and material improvements and proposing corresponding updates for official design specifications.
1985–1989	**Architectural Planner I, Department of Recreation, City of Avalon, New Jersey.** Assisted in conversion of military facilities to playgrounds in low-income neighborhoods.
	Supervised work teams formed to dismantle unsafe structures, salvage usable construction materials, and restore small buildings for use as maintenance facilities.
	Presented recreational equipment design proposals at a series of city council public sessions.

The Functional Résumé

Many experienced job candidates find that the most effective strategy of all is to focus their résumé entirely on their skills and achievements, minimizing the time factor. The functional résumé lets you place the skills and accomplishments you consider your greatest strengths in the most important position, regardless of when they occurred in your career. You can describe these factors

FUNCTIONAL RÉSUMÉ

Joan Durban
12 Poplar Ave.
Hope, Arkansas

Career goal: A position in senior management in a regional architectural firm.

Education: Columbia School of Architecture, M.S. Architectural Engineering, 1985.
Colorado School of Mines, B.S. Civil Engineering, 1982.

Experience

Engineering: Planned foundation and utility layouts for five subdivisions of publicly funded rural low-income housing near Hope, Arkansas, representing business of $1,300,000 annually.

Developed a design strategy that increased by 225 percent the number of concrete slabs that could be poured using the standard set of forms, thereby reducing project overhead by 26 percent.

Developed third-generation subroutines to improve corrosion protection in slab foundation hookups.

Assisted in updating specifications for bonding materials for use in city utility conduit assembly in Little Rock, Arkansas.

Assisted in various engineering aspects of deactivation of military base in Avalon, New Jersey, adaptation of facilities for use as low-income housing, and conversion of former equipment maintenance yards and surplus equipment into playgrounds and playground equipment for low-income neighborhoods.

Administration: Initiated the use of state-of-the-art CAD software into planning unit of engineering company, allowing a 66 percent

in greater depth than in a chronological résumé, even describing skills that you used in various combinations of jobs over the years. You can describe in several categories the various tasks involved in a single job assignment.

The actual dates of employment are listed at the end of the résumé. After all, which is more important for your potential employer to know: the dates you started and left your former jobs, or the individual skills you learned and

reduction in time required to develop new floor plans, reducing overall cost to company by 11 percent.

Researched and proposed purchase of new computer and networking hardware to allow maximum benefit of new CAD software.

Researched availability of new technologies for cutting costs of maintaining, repairing, upgrading, and expanding municipal sewer system in Little Rock, Arkansas.

Supervised teams of 3 to 5 civil engineers in slab foundation planning and design process.

Budgeting: Saved over $680,000 in public funds for the City of Little Rock, Arkansas, by revising outdated material specifications and recommending use of new materials and utility trenching technologies.

Achieved $275,000 in overall annual cost reduction for planning department of engineering company.

Training: Instructed and tutored 7 staff engineers and engineer trainees in use of state-of-the-art CAD software for foundation layout planning.

Assisted in training and orientation of new employees assigned to civil engineering office of Department of Recreation of the City of Avalon, New Jersey.

Work History

1992–present: **Assistant to the Chief Engineer,** Homes, Inc., Hope, Arkansas.

1989–1992: **Planner,** Engineering Division, City of Little Rock, Arkansas.

1985–1989: **Architectural Planner I**, Department of Recreation, City of Avalon, New Jersey.

developed over the years as you moved from one situation to another? Obviously what you can do is more to the point than when you last did it, or for whom, or in what city.

Other items that you might wish to mention in your résumé include community involvement, volunteer work, hobbies, interests, and a statement that references will be furnished upon request. These items should be career related or reflect your career interests as much as possible. Suppose you're applying for a job in safety training and your hobbies include weekend motorcycle racing; unless you're the motorcross safety officer, the less said, the better.

YOUR BRIDGE TO THE INTERVIEW

Remember this: The résumé that you send to your prospective employers will be the first item they see that is the product of your work and that represents you and your work history; make it look good. It will probably be a major guide for asking you questions and finding out more about you. Make it easy and interesting for the interviewer to develop these questions.

Your résumé may also be in the interviewer's hand when she picks up the telephone to call you and arrange an interview. When you think about what you will say and how you will present yourself on the telephone—the subject of the next chapter—you may find it useful to have your résumé handy. Keep it near the phone.

CHAPTER 11

BUILD YOUR
TELEPHONE
CONFIDENCE

When I was a child, I once asked my father how to hit a home run. "Here is how to hit a home run," he said. "First, you have to show up for practice. Then, in the game, you pick up a bat and stand at the plate, ready to swing. You have to keep your eye on the ball. When you hit the ball, run as fast as you can to first base. If things are clear then you might be able to run to second base. Keep alert as you are running around the bases. Sometimes you'll be able to run around all the bases, but that only happens once in a while. In order to hit a home run, you have to practice and be ready to swing at a lot of pitches."

At the time, I felt a little sorry that I had even asked the question. I didn't want to know *that* much about hitting home runs. But the message stuck with me: To arrive, you have to make the trip.

TELEPHONE ROULETTE

Once, while serving as a personnel consultant for a life insurance agency in Memphis, I was asked to help a frustrated young insurance agent named Tom find another job. As his general manager put it, "In six months the only policy he sold was to his mother."

We began his job search by setting goals and developing lists of potential employers. However, after two weeks of list building, Tom had not turned up a single interview. Although he was bright and intellectually curious, he was more prone to contemplation than action.

My goal for our next meeting was to help him see the importance of taking action on his plans. When he arrived, I told him that we were going to do telephone prospecting.

First, I asked him to write a short script to introduce himself and explain why he should get an interview. The script was general enough to cover almost any situation, but specific about what he could do for an employer. We practiced the script until he felt he could converse naturally and easily about its main points. Then we put it aside.

Next, I asked him to give me his trust—a "blank contract" based on my sincere interest in his success. I wanted him to try a novel approach that I believed would immediately get him interviews and reward him for taking action. He agreed.

I explained that were going to play "Telephone Roulette." Following my instructions, he flipped through the yellow pages at random, and blindly put his finger on a company name. It was the name of a paint store. "Call and get an interview," I said. He seemed a little shocked, but he had promised to do what I asked.

Using his script with practiced ease, he managed to arrange an interview for a supervisor's job in the paint store. He riffled through the yellow pages again and got a job referral from the attorney he had randomly selected. Then he called the metropolitan sports complex and got an interview with the City of Memphis. Every time he called, he got results. He was amazed: "All I have to do is call!"

Tom soon realized that his reluctance to use the telephone was his main problem as an insurance agent and that he could improve his skills and keep his job. Even so, he decided to keep prospecting for a job that would better fit his own needs. He got a good job offer within two weeks. When I saw him later, he told me that he was happy with his work and in line for a promotion.

SIXTY-SECOND TELEPHONE SCRIPT GUIDE

Salutation; 5 seconds

Hello, I am _____. Thank you for the opportunity to speak with you.

To refresh your memory, we met at _____.

Is this a good time to talk?

Establish the reason for the call; 10 seconds

I am calling about _____.

I was referred to you by _____.

Could you tell me what type of skills you are looking for?

Establish your qualifications; 20 seconds

I have worked as a _____.

I have experience in _____.

My degree is in _____.

Make benefit statements; 10 seconds to 2 minutes

I am skilled in _____.

I was trained in _____.

I have completed classes in _____.

Ask for an interview; 5 seconds

I would like to ask for an interview. Is there a time that would be convenient for you?

Wrap up the conversation; 10 seconds

Thank you for the opportunity of speaking with you.

Is there anything special I should prepare to talk about in the interview?

Can you give me directions to where the interview will take place?

I'm looking forward to meeting with you.

CALL RELUCTANCE

Over the years I have worked with many people who had call reluctance—salespeople who weren't realizing their potential and job search candidates who waited passively for opportunities, among others. Low self-esteem, fear of rejection, and other factors kept them from picking up the telephone and placing themselves in the way of opportunity. They rationalized their reluctance with any number of excuses.

Telephone Roulette is a practical way to overcome these fears—and an important tool in getting interviews. Being able to use the telephone effectively is one of the most valuable career skills that you can have. The telephone is a contact multiplier: it lets you present yourself to many more people than you can talk with in person. Learn to use it effectively, to state clearly and succinctly in a series of calls how the organization can benefit by interviewing you face-to-face, and you will easily survive the telephone screening process that many organizations use.

PHONE TO GET INTERVIEWS

A lot of people say they like talking with people but avoid using the telephone. If you're this kind of telephobe, you're hurting your job chances. The more contacts you can make, the more high-potential interviews you'll land. In a month of hard work, you can meet twenty people in person—or you can make four hundred telephone calls.

How, you may well ask, can I learn to use the phone the way the experts do, the ones who are successful at making all those contacts? The answer: Watch the pros. Visit a professionally managed customer-service call center—one that both receives calls from customers and makes telemarketing sales calls. Watch a service representative handle a customer or a prospect. Observe how his office is arranged, what resources and supplies he keeps at hand. You'll begin to understand what you may be doing wrong, and you'll learn some telephone techniques that can help you get in for an interview.

Here are some of the things I've observed in my visits to the best of these call centers, and some lessons you can draw from them.

- Each person in a call center works in a controlled environment, organized to make calls go smoothly. Background noise is low; the person on the other end of the line will hear no photocopier copying, no trucks trundling by, no one yelling from another room. There's no clutter of papers to rattle; phone lists and note pads are kept near the phone, along with half a dozen sharpened pencils. The telephone has a headset, so it's never dropped. What does this tell you about making calls next to the TV in your living room, where the kids are playing video games? Lock your-self in your study before calling contacts—and organize your desk.

- The service representative is easy to contact; the customer never gets a busy signal. The person who answers the phone is the person the customer needs to talk to. If you expect to be called at home, on a phone that you share, answer the phone yourself whenever possible. Otherwise, get an answering machine, record as professional a message as possible, and ask everyone in your household to let the machine answer all calls.

- Why are all these service reps smiling? Because it makes them sound friendly and accessible. Keep a positive attitude when calling contacts; a pessimistic attitude can too easily be transmitted over phone lines. To help you personalize the conversation, develop a positive visual image of the person you are talking with. If necessary, find an appealing magazine ad with a diverse group of people in it, and look at the smiling faces as you talk.

- Telemarketers and service reps use "call scripts" for guidance—a different script for each situation. They never read the script to the customer; it's mainly a training tool that gets them accustomed to dealing with a variety of situations smoothly and automatically. You should develop call scripts to guide the way you talk to receptionists, personnel recruiters, and managers.

- Each call leads to personalized action. The salesperson makes a sale, gets the customer interested in learning more, or at least tries to end the call on a friendly note. The service rep either solves a customer problem or helps the customer understand it. Sometimes he follows through via letter or fax. Learn from this. Have a cover letter ready to adapt and send to your target; be ready to fax or mail your résumé immediately.

Keep in mind that, for all practical purposes, the interview begins with your first telephone contact. Many interviewers will begin to rate your professionalism and interpersonal skills according to how well you conduct yourself on the phone. Take a hard look at your telephone skills, and prepare yourself to build a good first impression.

THE WORLD'S GREATEST EXCUSES NOT TO CALL

- Someone may be trying to call me about a job.
- I need to eat first to build up my energy.
- I only have about twenty minutes.
- My dog is barking now.
- I already have an interview set up.
- I am going to wait and see if I get engaged.
- I want to loose five pounds before I interview.
- I haven't had a vacation in ten years.
- I am already too stressed out.
- I need to buy a word processor first so I can do letters.
- The interviewer is probably at lunch.
- The newspaper said that business was bad now.
- They wouldn't be interested in me.
- I don't want to work in that part of town.
- One of my friends already tried to get a job there.
- I need to get a haircut before I start interviewing.
- It's Friday—nobody will be there.
- I need to build my telephone file first.
- I don't have my stationary yet.
- I need to get a new suit.

WHAT TO SAY

How do you choose precisely the words to say over the phone that will win you an interview? Stay focused on one central fact: You must be prepared to help the recruiter believe that it is to her organization's benefit to grant you an interview.

Being prepared means not only being ready to communicate key facts about your qualifications, but also cultivating a telephone presence that is

- confident, but not arrogant
- prepared, but not mechanical
- professional, but not cold
- assertive, but not aggressive
- friendly, but not cavalier
- available, but not needy

YEAH-BUT

Forget it! I hate using the telephone.

COACH'S COMEBACK

Keep trying. It's a very important skill, and you can learn to tolerate it. Think of a time in your past when circumstances forced you to learn something; apply that understanding to your current situation. If you don't learn to be effective with the telephone, you will dramatically reduce the number of contacts that you can make. In a tight job market, someone who is willing to use the phone will get your job!

For getting across your qualifications efficiently and effectively, there's no substitute for a telephone script. Writing a script makes you think about exactly what you wish to communicate. It can help you discover and eliminate words or phrases that might give the recruiter the wrong impression about you. It helps you project a positive image of yourself, along with your summary of what you can do for the organization. Once you have developed and polished it, your telephone script will give you confidence—a calm self-assurance that will help your contact realize you are the kind of person she wants to interview.

Most contact calls last only a few minutes, just long enough to establish rapport, state your qualifications for the job, and arrange an interview if possible. Your basic script should be concise; don't try to keep the recruiter on the line longer than she wants. Sometimes, however, if you've raised the interviewer's interest, you may find your call turning into a telephone mini-interview. You need to be prepared for this contingency, ready to communicate on any aspect of your career, to describe such things as

- your educational experiences and special training
- your employment history
- the kinds of jobs that you are qualified for
- special qualifications for the job you are applying for
- your knowledge of the organization's work
- your understanding of the organization's culture and values

COACH'S TIP

Keep your résumé next to the phone. It will prompt you as you respond to questions, enabling you to be specific on your work history and skills.

There are many ways you can communicate these things on the telephone, some more effective than others. When you prepare for an in-person interview, you anticipate what you will be asked about, and plan your response in the form of detailed skill-benefit questions. When you plan your first telephone contact with your target organization, you should also try to anticipate how the conversation will go, but prepare to respond more succinctly. Formulate answers that are practical and to the point.

Using the telephone script guide on page 165, write out what you need to say to get invited in for an interview.

PREPARE FOR THE TELEPHONE INTERVIEW

Many organizations are beginning to use the telephone interview as a standard part of the screening process. This use of the telephone goes well beyond the contact call, even the mini-interview call. A telephone interview covers much of the same territory as a traditional face-to-face interview; you may not meet an interviewer in person until late in the selection process, after you have been selected as a finalist.

From the employer's standpoint, the telephone interview is effective for eliminating unqualified candidates with minimal commitment of time and resources to assess their skills. It is also fast and easy to administer.

For the candidate, a telephone interview has its advantages and disadvantages. It is often unpredictable; you don't know when, or even if, you'll be called. The telephone rings, you answer, and the interview begins. (In my opinion, a considerate interviewer will call ahead and arrange a time for a formal telephone interview.) By the same token, it doesn't much matter whether you've shaved or put on makeup.

SAMPLE TELEPHONE INTERVIEW QUESTIONS
FOR A BOOKKEEPER IN A REAL ESTATE COMPANY

1. What aspects of your work experience would relate to bookkeeping for a real estate company?

2. What experience have you had with double-entry bookkeeping?

3. How often do you need to reconcile depreciation schedules with your balance sheet?

4. What types of accounting information do you feel you should immediately report to your manager?

5. What types of accounting software packages do you have experience with?

6. What experience have you had in reconciling multiple bank accounts?

7. What experience have you had in reading amortization schedules?

8. Describe the key aspects of planning that a bookkeeper should carry out.

9. Describe the payroll procedures you've worked with.

10. What is the bookkeeper's role in maintaining rental records?

11. Tell me how to develop financial statements that account for assets, liabilities, revenue, and expenses.

12. How do you develop quarterly payroll tax forms?

13. Explain the procedures for administrating medical and disability insurance.

14. Describe how to maintain retirement plans.

15. What information should the bookkeeper compile for the tax accountant?

Your first warning might be a phone call that begins with, "Is this a good time?" A well-prepared interviewer would then begin by reviewing a job description (if available) and your résumé or application; he might indicate specifically why you are being considered as a candidate to be interviewed in person. He would identify areas of your experience that might qualify you for further consideration.

A telephone interviewer usually spends ten to thirty minutes asking questions about your education, job skills, technical knowledge, and work experience. This kind of interview typically involves less emphasis on your performance skills, such as teamwork, organization, and leadership, which most interviewers prefer to evaluate in person.

Once in a while you may experience an "ambush" interview. That is, the interviewer may try to catch you off guard to see how you respond to questions under pressure. I consider this a rather low-grade way to assess your job skills, and would doubt the objectivity and competence of any interviewer using this technique.

Nevertheless, prepare for an ambush interview the same way you would prepare for a professional telephone interview:

- Organize your household so you can control who answers your phone. Specifically, do not allow children or adults with average telephone presence to answer your line. If necessary, keep your own phone locked up.

- Use an answering machine to screen your calls. Answer calls from the recruiter immediately; call others back.

- Keep your résumé and copies of all correspondence near the telephone so you can refer quickly to information you sent the employer.

- Breathe deeply before you pick up the phone. Excitement, or a sprint to the phone, can make you short-winded.

During the telephone interview, be as specific as possible in answering questions. Prepare by formulating SHARE answers, just as you would for an in-person interview. On the phone, you have an extra advantage: you can keep a crib sheet handy to help you remember all the wonderful answers that you might have forgotten in a regular interview. Don't read them over the phone, though; just jog your memory, then talk as though you were looking the interviewer in the eye.

One final point about telephone talk: Never assume that you know what's happening on the other end of the line. While you're sitting there disheveled in your coffee-stained T-shirt, you may think you're having a heart-to-heart chat with a person who looks a lot like you and shares your feelings and beliefs. In truth, your remarks may be overheard by any number of people who happen to near the speakerphone, some of whom may take offense at your witty remark about people in blue suits.

UNSEEN RAPPORT

The important point to keep in mind is that you need as much advance good will as possible to smooth your way into a favorable interview. Once you've prepared yourself to communicate your fascinating career story, gained favorable attention with your well-constructed résumé, and charmed everybody with your easy telephone manner, you've already gone a long way toward one of your most desirable objectives—gaining an advocate inside the company.

CHAPTER 12

CULTIVATE YOUR ADVOCATE

In my years as an interviewer, I considered part of my job to be protecting candidates and organizations from partisan politics—that is, helping to select the most qualified candidate regardless of personal connections or biases. Nevertheless, I soon became aware of how often the candidate's success depended on behind-the-scenes advocacy, and came to understand that the advocate can do a great service for both the employer and the candidate by matching a highly qualified person with a crucial employer need.

Your advocate can be a person on the selection team, elsewhere within the organization, or even outside the organization—in any case, someone whose reputation, credibility, and influence can sway the decision in favor of hiring you. The advocate must know your skills and character and be able to describe what you could do for the organization. He or she can speak for you when you're not there, answer questions about you, and help communicate important information about your skills.

School ties have long been a natural source of advocates. Pledges to college fraternities and sororities are assigned "big brothers" and "big sisters" to speak up for the pledge in members-only meetings. A candidate for a university teaching job is typically brought to the faculty's attention and introduced by a champion who knows the individual's work. An advocate for a corporate job candidate is often someone who went to school with the candidate and can speak for the candidate's skills, potential, and work habits. You should consider every training experience an opportunity to find advocates for yourself, as well as to become an advocate for others.

Of course, any behind-the-scenes subjective input into the selection process is vulnerable to abuse. A real problem with advocacy is that it can be discriminatory. The phrase "old boys' club" comes to mind. When the most powerful advocates share the same values and experiences, capable people with different backgrounds tend to be ignored, or worse, excluded. Taken to extremes, ardent advocacy can place people in positions for which they are not suited; the result can be disaster for both the organization and the employee.

HOW TO FIND ADVOCATES

If you don't know anyone in the organization you're trying to get hired into, how do you get someone to be your advocate? It's not as hard as you might think. In a way, this question is backward. When you're scouting out employment prospects, sometimes it works better to think in terms of an advocate first, the organization second. That is, if you can first get in touch with an individual who is impressed by your credentials or otherwise favorably inclined toward you, that person may be able to steer you to a good job opportunity and help you maneuver through the process of getting an interview and a job offer.

Start with Who You Know

The foremost and most efficient way to gain advocates is to contact people you have met, communicated with, or come to know in your work.

- Review the business cards you've saved over the years. Contact each person with the objective of gaining job leads.

- Compile a list of vendors and suppliers you have worked with in your jobs. Call and ask for ideas on places that need your skills.

- Contact a former employer or co-worker whom you pleased, and ask for an interview. If an interview is not forthcoming, ask for referrals.

YEAH-BUT

Do I just ask somebody to be my advocate? That seems awfully pushy.

COACH'S COMEBACK

You're right. It's not that simple. Your best approach is to identify potential advocates and ask them questions about the job, the organization, and the organization's products or services. If the individual begins to give you encouragement, you have a possible advocate. If you don't get much response, keep looking.

- Use your time after working hours and on weekends to do contract work with business associates and prospective employers, taking care that there is no conflict of interest.

- Volunteer to do unpaid work for professional associates who might be interested in hiring you later.

Broaden Your Circle of Professional Contacts

After you have gotten in touch with people you know professionally, expand your efforts to include individuals you have not met but who might know of your work, who work in the same field as you, or who might otherwise be interested in your professional qualifications were they to learn of them.

- Use the *Wall Street Journal* and other business publications to develop a list of companies with a high price/earnings ratio. These are probably high-growth organizations that are actively recruiting candidates for a variety of jobs. Find the names of key people in these organizations.

- Go to the reception area of an organization you would like to join and ask for a recruiting professional by name. Indicate that you would like to wait until you can personally give him or her a résumé.

- At a meeting of a professional organization, ask the program chairperson to let you make a twenty-second announcement of your availability. When the time is right, stand up and introduce your skills to the audience.

> ### COACH'S TIP
>
> Assume that busy people in responsible jobs do have the time to help you. Successful people typically return their calls and respond to inquiries. You may, of course, get only a referral to another part of the organization, but that referral can open a door for you.

- Most professional organizations have employment/placement services at their national conventions. Put yourself on the "available for interview" list and attend the convention.

- Take out an advertisement in your professional association's newsletter. Include a brief description of your education and skills and ask for an interview.

- Take part-time work in a temporary-placement firm, and impress an employer well enough to earn an interview for full-time employment.

Target Individuals Outside Your Professional Circle

There are key individuals in influential positions who may have an interest in seeing that you are gainfully employed. These may be people you do not know personally and who are not associated directly with your professional interests, but who may nevertheless be motivated to help you find employment opportunities.

- Write to your congressional representatives, explaining what you do and where you would like to work. You will receive a call from a congressional aide who can be very helpful.

- Arrange for an interview with your banker. Present your résumé, review your skills, and ask for interview leads, with a personal introduction if possible.

- Ask a stockbroker who is making money in your field. Then ask if he or she can help you get an introduction.

- Contact your favorite college professor(s), review your work experiences, and ask for referrals to employers. A personal introduction by the professor is of great value.

Mass Market Yourself

Another way to approach the problem is to think the way major merchandisers do. Communicate with people you know outside of work, or even people you do not know but who share some potential common interest. The more people you can contact, the more interviews you'll get. Sure, you may get responses from only a small percentage, but a small fraction of a large number can be enough to give you a choice of several opportunities. Once you have an entrée into the organization, then you can begin to cultivate advocates.

- Get a listing of government job openings. Complete all the paperwork for your application and be prepared to wait for a phone call.

- Drive down the busiest street in your town. Make a list of the organizations that seem to be extra busy and contact them.

- Walk through a local shopping mall and identify the products and companies that seem to do well. Contact the successful organizations that appeal to you.

- Contact each person on your holiday mailing list. Ask for referrals for the specific type of job you are looking for.

- From your high school and college yearbooks, develop a list of people to call. The odds are that you know several successful people who will be glad to help you.

YEAH-BUT

I feel that mass marketing myself is too impersonal. I just don't believe that it works.

COACH'S COMEBACK

Wrong! Mass marketing can work for you. I recently conducted a seminar for thirty-two recruiters who will fill about three thousand positions in one year for one organization. Their primary sources for new hires are newspaper ads, résumés, and referrals. You may have to make five hundred contacts in a month—but the right job is well worth the effort.

- Call all of your neighbors, explain that you are out of work, and ask for interview leads.

- Ask the people in your exercise or cooking class for referrals. This may steer you to opportunities outside your current business network.

- Take evening classes to improve your professional skills. Ask the instructor and classmates for interview leads.

- Display your résumé on the bulletin board at your child-care center. Have your business cards tacked under your résumé to make it easy for someone to call.

- Put your résumé on the Internet or an on-line service.

FINDING YOUR CHAMPION

Following are some accounts by people of diverse backgrounds who have told me of their real-life experiences in cultivating advocates. These stories are very revealing; every person I asked was able to recount a positive experience—even people from groups that are regularly discriminated against.

"I got to know the college placement officer in my college fairly well because we shared classes together. When I graduated I didn't have a clue about where I could get a job. So my placement officer gave me the name of the recruiter for the convention bureau and told me that I must speak to this person. I was so persistent in calling that I thought, This lady is going to strangle me for bothering her. I learned to get my message in quick. Eventually, the recruiter referred me to where I work today. She said that I was persistent and that seemed to be a plus—but the real thing is that she was willing to speak for me and persuade the company to interview me." S. K.

"I applied for a job, took a battery of tests, and completed a one-and-a-half-hour interview. I was told that I would know something within a week. When I didn't get a call, I went ahead and took another job. It was horrible. The second day on my new job I got a call to come in for my second interview at the place I wanted to work. The person who called me remembered who I was and was able to explain to everyone why I should still be interviewed. He became my advocate, because I had to overcome reservations about my commitment based on my willingness to leave the job I had just started. This is where I work today." W. S.

THE POWER OF PREPARATION

The above suggestions are far from an exhaustive list of actions you can take to acquire and benefit from advocates. In fact, consider them a starter list; reading and following through on some of them should cause you to think of many other resources that I've failed to mention, that only you would know about. Pursue every idea. Even a blind alley has an end, and you may meet someone there who has gone the same way and learned something he can teach you.

Set your goal at what may seem like an unrealistic number. If you can do a mass mailing of five hundred résumés with personalized letters to targeted individuals, you can expect to get from five to ten interview opportunities over

"My job was eliminated just before I had my second child, so my severance package allowed me to take about eight months off work. Instead of taking a full-time job, I started taking job assignments with a temporary-placement firm. They sent me to all kinds of places. It really gave me a complete view of what the job market was like for my skills. Then I was recruited to accept a full-time job by the person I worked for at my last assignment. He was my advocate to his boss, who had the final decision on hiring me. After I got the job, he told me that he liked to hire people based on their performance as a temporary." A. B.

"After leaving the air force, I completed commercial flight training. But I decided to not pursue an airline job because they wouldn't be hiring for some time. When I was being considered for a security director position, I discovered that the hiring manager had also been in the air force. That worked to my benefit. But the big advantage came because I was able to get a colonel who knew my work to call for me. He was the best advocate I could have asked for. I got the job with lightning speed." G. W.

"When I found that my department at the bank was to be eliminated, I went through the yellow pages and found the names of potential employers in my field. When I started making calls, I had my little speech set up—it was quick and clean. One of the people who returned my call explained that he knew that he was overdrawn and that it was already taken care of. When I explained why I was calling, we both had a big laugh. Then I got an interview and the job I have had for eight years." A. P.

several months. That may not sound like a lot, but since you've targeted your mailings, you may find that these few are genuine opportunities for you.

You have now made all the basic preparations you need for maximizing your chances of success in an interview. From now on, it's reality time. The next part of this book will describe for you what does and can happen once you sit down for the interview, and shows you how to handle the expected and the not-so-expected.

BE NUMBER THREE

I've heard many people say your chances are best if you're the third candidate interviewed. I never put much stock in this idea until I began regularly teaching interviewing to interviewers. Many of them said they liked to have three candidates to interview: one was a no, another a maybe, and the third a hire.

Still I remained skeptical. I had often interviewed six candidates in one day without finding a single one that I would hire. On the other hand, sometimes I recommended the first person I interviewed. Why? Because I always compared the candidate's responses to job-related selection criteria.

Many interviewers don't use job-related selection criteria; instead, they compare candidates with one another. Three seems to be the ideal number for these comparisons; two is not enough, and four seems like extra work.

Most interviewers also need time to warm up. With candidate one, they're having their first cup of coffee and limbering up their interview technique. Candidate number two affords additional practice and builds the interviewer's confidence. With the third candidate, the interviewer is awake, relaxed, attentive, comfortable, and eager to make a decision.

So you may have a slight advantage if you're the third candidate of the day. This is far from being an absolute; many other factors influence a competent interviewer's decision. It's also an area where you have little control. You can't ask the interviewer to let you be candidate number three. But if you're asked which time would be most convenient—8:00, 9:30, or 11:00—pick eleven.

The true advantage comes from being aware that many interviewers need time to warm up. A greater advantage comes when your responses to questions match the selection criteria and are better than those of your competitors.

PART FOUR

PRESENT YOUR CASE

You've done everything you can to prepare yourself for the interview. You've identified your skills, connected them with potential benefits for your employer, rehearsed answering all kinds of questions, skill-related and otherwise. You've thought of your career in terms of a movie or a legend, put together an effective and influential résumé, presented yourself well in telephone conversations with your target, and gained an advocate inside the organization.

By now you should be feeling fairly confident about your chances of getting a job offer.

An acquaintance of mine once told me, "I'm a whiz at getting ready for an interview. I write out and rehearse every major point I want to make, I get friends to ask me tough questions, I review every detail and all the facts and numbers I can think of. I'm ready for any question anyone could possibly ask me.

"But when I get there and sit down across the table from the interviewer, why am I still so nervous that I can hardly sit still? I've been calmer getting shot at in combat."

In that last sentence, my friend answered his own question. Sure, you can plan and plan, but when it comes to the crunch, the worst time is after you've finished planning and before you've begun to act. Now you have a better picture of what can happen, including what can go wrong. Sure, you know how to respond appropriately and well, but will you? You don't know for sure until you do act. Then it gets better.

You are now at that stage. You're as prepared as you can get, but you can't act on it yet. Only after the interview begins will all that preparation kick in. Then, as soon as you begin responding to the interviewer's greetings and questions, you'll find that your preparations will lead you to say the right thing at the right time.

Of course, the interview has a dynamic all its own that you can't really prepare for in the same way you prepare to answer to the facts of your case. Each interview has its own feel, its own energy, its own line of progress as it develops from moment to moment, driven by a mix of questions, responses, moods, prejudices, courtesies, and appearances.

That's what this next part of the book is about—the moment-to-moment dramatic action of the interview itself. You'll learn in chapter 13 about how you and the interviewer both benefit from establishing and maintaining an easy rapport. Chapters 14 and 15 will give you tips on how to avoid offending the interviewer with your appearance, your attitude, your manner, and your mouth. And chapter 16 gives you pointers on what happens when you're sent to see the corporate psychologist (don't worry; it's probably a good sign).

RAPPORT, AND HOW TO GET IT

The interviewer strides into the room and sits across the table from you. "Just who are you, anyway?" he demands.

Are you in the wrong room? Are the police on the way? Are your pants on backward? Who is this hostile person, and how are you supposed to respond to him?

Perhaps some of these questions went through the mind of the unfortunate candidate who was actually confronted this way. It startled me, too, and I was just there to observe. I had underestimated just how bad an untrained interviewer, even an intelligent and successful sales manager, could be.

Rather than attending a regular workshop, the interviewer had retained me to spend a day observing him, giving him feedback, and demonstrating my approach to interviewing. I pulled no punches. I told the interviewer that his technique was haughty, abrupt, and presumptive. It would made a good candidate regret showing up and put the average candidate on the defensive. It was a bad question and a bad way to start the interview, I said. What was the value of being so abrupt with the candidate?

The interviewer explained that, in his opinion, an effective salesperson had to be able to "think on his feet." The "stress question" was meant to test the candidate's ability to deal with unruly customers—the way the interviewer had learned to do. A good salesperson should be able to shrug off rude, offensive comments, to "get the business, whatever the circumstances"—like the interviewer.

This interviewer was making the "cloning error"—looking for someone like himself in the belief that his way was the only way. Not only was his pet theory a poor basis for evaluating a candidate, it led to a disastrous beginning for an interview. It set a confrontational tone from the start, a move that immediately put the candidate on the defensive, killed rapport, and made it more difficult to get objective information about his real qualifications.

You may walk into the interview and find yourself facing just such an unpromising beginning. If you do, treat it as a test of your interpersonal skills. Stay calm. Take a beat or two. Think carefully about your answer. Look the interviewer in the eye, smile, and reply with a few well-chosen words. The way you take command of the situation will not go unnoticed; in fact, it may be exactly what the interviewer is looking for.

A COMMON INTEREST

A good interviewer has at least one interest in common with you—achieving rapport. The interviewer builds rapport to make you feel comfortable with sharing information about yourself. Your purpose in building rapport is to get the interviewer to like you and to feel that you are a good candidate for the job.

Rapport building is near the top of the list in virtually every book on interviewing. In our own Behavioral Interviewing® seminar, we show interviewers how to ask rapport-building questions—casual, open-ended questions designed to help the candidate feel comfortable talking—before getting down to more substantive questions. In any type of interview, you should respond in a friendly way to the interviewer's rapport-building gestures by picking up and elaborating on the conversation to indicate that you are relaxed, confident, and cooperative.

Good rapport progresses through three phases: attaining, maintaining, and sustaining. Attaining rapport takes only a few minutes, but an important few minutes; your goal is to create a positive first impression by how you look

---

COACH'S TIP

Don't forget to smile. You may be the kind of person who wears a concerned, serious look when dealing with something as weighty as an interview. By smiling, at least upon first meeting the interviewer, you can contribute to rapport.

---

and act, and to follow the interviewer's conversational lead. The rapport you build in the first phase tends to set, like gelatin. Maintaining rapport then becomes mostly a matter of avoiding big mistakes that can shatter the mold and turn off the interviewer. Sustaining rapport is mainly the task of finishing the interview gracefully and leaving behind a good impression.

ATTAINING RAPPORT

This first stage of rapport building lasts only five minutes or so (my rule of thumb), but the result, whether successful or unsuccessful, usually dominates the rest of the interview. Obviously, getting off on the right foot is your immediate goal. If you do, maintaining rapport is easier; if not, you spend a lot of energy trying to dig yourself out of a hole.

First Impressions

One way or another, you're going to make a first impression. Make it work for you, not against you. The car you arrive in, the shoes you are wearing, the way you walk into the room, your first remark—all convey a certain nonverbal impression to the interviewer. Make it a positive one; mind the details.

Research suggests that interviewers tend to search for negative information and come to quick conclusions about candidates based on information presented early in the interview. In one early study, 85 percent of interviewers' decisions were based on information from the first four minutes of the interview. A single unfavorable rating led to a reject decision 90 percent of the time.[1]

Many executives believe that an interviewer should be able to size up a candidate quickly. In one survey they were asked, "How long does it take interviewers to make decisions about the job suitability of the candidate?" Seventy-four percent answered five minutes or less, 17 percent said six to sixty minutes, and only 9 percent said more than an hour.[2] These beliefs, right or wrong, lend a certain validity to first impressions and gut feelings. Of course, a well-trained interviewer will avoid making snap decisions, but you can't count on having a good interviewer. Your best strategy is to prepare for the worst, and consider yourself lucky if you draw a skilled interviewer.

These results lead to clear recommendations. Pay particular attention to how you look, what you do, and what you say on first meeting the interviewer. Use common sense; interviewers and organizations differ, and standard rules may not apply. You won't always be expected to wear a business suit; offering a handshake could be a mistake. For each interview situation, make a conscious choice about how to present yourself.

Positive Visual Impact

Within the first few seconds of meeting the interviewer, you have already communicated a visual message. If you've prepared yourself well, your message will be that you are a skilled professional and a good team player with the skills for doing the job well. This message is more likely to be communicated if you

- inspect yourself before the interview by looking in a mirror;
- check that buttons, zippers, belts, and laces are correctly deployed;
- carry a planning calendar or a small briefcase with work samples; and
- have a résumé ready (not folded).

The Handshake

Should you offer to shake hands? The tradition has been to extend your hand and give a firm, confident handshake. But this may be the wrong approach in some situations. Some cultures view touching as too intimate. Many women consider a handshake too much of a male tradition. And some, like one interviewer I met, are concerned about germs:

"I interview sixteen college students a day. Many of them don't carry handkerchiefs and sneeze on their hands. Odds are I'm going to be exposed to the flu several times during a recruiting week. Also, I don't want to give Candidate Six the germs from Candidate Five when I shake hands. So I generally try to avoid shaking hands by making an open gesture of where the candidate should sit. It doesn't work all the time, so I regularly wash my hands between interviews."

A handshake today is a judgment call. If the interviewer extends a hand, go for it. Otherwise, smile big and wait for the invitation.

LOOK AT YOURSELF IN THE MIRROR

Many years ago I interviewed a recent college graduate who was bright, candid, and charming, and well qualified for the job. At the time I thought it rare and refreshing to see all of these qualities combined in one person.

He was also very fortunate to have an interviewer who could look beyond his image. His black shoes were muddy; his belt was brown; his suspenders had flowers. (I knew even then you didn't wear suspenders with a belt.) He was in dire need of someone else's experienced eye.

When it comes to first impressions, I try to be critical of myself and forgiving of the candidate. I strive to credit the content of candidate's answers and ignore subjective negative impressions. Still, I was bothered by this candidate's loose tie, mesmerized by the inch of shirt I could see above it.

I could ignore many of the details of his image. But I kept asking myself, Why hadn't he looked in the mirror before the interview? If he had, he might have done something to make himself look better.

This story ends happily. I overcame my reservations and recommended hiring him on the basis of his knowledge, skills, and intellect. The employer was astute enough to look beyond first impressions; the candidate was offered the job. But the outcome could have been very different with another interviewer or another organization. His failure to look at himself with a critical eye could have been an expensive career mistake.

Your Positioning Statement

By arriving well groomed, well dressed, and on time, you've communicated your first positive statement about yourself—and you haven't yet said a word. Your next move is to speak, to make a positioning statement. The first thing you say should include three components: (1) the interviewer's name, (2) your appreciation for the interview, and (3) an indication that you're ready to cooperate.

Pick one of the following examples that feels close to what you would naturally say, and put it into your own words. Then practice it.

- "Dr. Green, it's a pleasure to have this opportunity to be with you today. I'm especially eager to share my skills in _____ with you."

- "Mr. Smith, thank you for allowing me to interview with you today. I want you to know up front that I am excited about letting you get to know me and my skills."

- "Ms. Jones, I appreciate your spending time with me today. I will attempt to be as thorough as possible in working with you during our interview."

It is usually best to first address the interviewer with Mr., Ms., or an academic title such as Dr. If the interviewer prefers to use given names, then she will invite you to do so.

Some Dos and Don'ts

The first moments of an interview are sometimes awkward; you don't know quite what to say, and if the interviewer doesn't put you at ease immediately with a bit of banter, you may be tempted to say the first thing that pops into your head. This can be a mistake. It's better to allow a little silence while you get comfortable and compose yourself. And here's a succinct list of things you probably shouldn't mention:

- Don't ask about salary or benefits.
- Don't refer to problems finding the office.
- Don't speak negatively about travel arrangements.
- Don't ask if the weather is always this bad.
- Don't say that you didn't get much sleep.
- Don't explain why you might do poorly in the interview.
- Don't volunteer why you lost your last job.
- Don't make reference to religion, politics, race, gender, age, or national origin.
- Don't bring up who you know in the organization.
- Don't try to "butter up" the interviewer by complimenting her appearance.
- Don't ask if you can show letters of recommendation.
- Don't make negative reference to anyone.
- Don't request refreshments that aren't offered.
- Don't inquire about lunch.

Having made your positioning statement, focus the conversation on the needs and interests of the interviewer:

- "Where would you like me to sit?"
- "Could you use another copy of my résumé?"
- "I've brought samples of my work that might interest you."
- "Do you have any concerns about special job or skill requirements that I can address?"
- "If you need any extra time with me, I can be very flexible."
- "Here's my business card for your future reference."

YEAH-BUT

One of my real strengths in my work search is the people I know. My contacts have a lot of pull in some big companies. You seem to be telling me not even to mention my contacts.

COACH'S COMEBACK

Not exactly. You're the best judge of whether it is to your advantage to drop a name or two. All I'm saying is that you need to be very careful with this approach. It can backfire. Instead, emphasize your skills, and if your contacts work to your advantage, they may be an added value in the interviewer's eyes.

The way these statements are phrased may not be exactly your style, but they illustrate the basic idea: ask questions and make offers to help the interviewer do his job.

MAINTAINING RAPPORT

Depending on how your first five minutes went, you will spend the next fifty minutes in either maintenance mode or breakout mode. You should hope it's the former. In breakout mode, you're trying to overcome a blunder, to correct something that went wrong at the beginning. In maintenance mode, all you have to do is avoid making serious errors that may cause the interviewer to question your social, personal, or professional judgment.

If you've come safely through the beginning of the interview, you'll spend most of your allotted hour maintaining rapport—unless you mess up and wander into a mine field. Every interviewer brings his own mine field with him, and if you stumble across one of the triggers, as naive candidates often do, you will find rapport suddenly withering, and you may not even know why.

Because many interviewers tend to overreact to negatives, trivial things can sink you. Something in your attitude, an innocent remark, an unconscious personal habit can rub the interviewer the wrong way and override all the good rapport and your excellent credentials. Most of these mine fields are known, so with a little study you can learn where they are and how to stay out of them.

Self-Aggrandizement

Many interviewers will give you ample opportunity to describe times when you used your skills successfully at work. Remember, though, that the interviewer may also want to evaluate your skills in teamwork and cooperation. If you dwell exclusively on your personal qualifications, you may seem self-absorbed. Downplaying your skills and successes often makes good sense; as a practical Texan once said, "The rooster who crows loudest gets the axe."

Acknowledge the contributions others have made to your successes. Avoid overusing the word "I"; substitute "we" wherever you can. This does not mean that you should talk in generalities; the interviewer will want to know exactly what steps you took in each situation. But the interviewer knows that others contributed to a successful outcome, and you should show that you are aware of this by describing your actions as a member of a team.

Low Confidence

Interviewing folklore holds that eye contact, a firm handshake, and erect posture were important signs of a candidate's self-confidence, social skills, and employability. In today's more sensitive, multicultural work environment, such indicators are questionable. Nevertheless, there is some merit in using them in moderation to demonstrate self-confidence without arrogance. Don't try to stare down the interviewer, but make eye contact while talking to him; when thinking out responses to questions, however, the most natural thing to do is to look to the side or into the distance. Shake hands only if the interviewer initiates the gesture—but be ready for it, and don't hesitate. Maintain good posture, but don't get rigid; sit straight, relax, and be as natural as possible.

Educational Arrogance

In my years of interviewing, I've met a graduate from a top business school who said that his M.B.A. was more valuable than a doctorate from a state-funded university; a candidate who based his purported intellectual superiority on a three-month executive development program; and several brand-new Ph.D.s who wished to be addressed as Doctor. Such attitudes tend to leave experienced interviewers wishing the candidate had taken a course in humility.

COACH'S TIP

BE DISCREET

When you and a potential employer are sizing each other up, you may encounter many situations when ethical considerations rule your actions. For instance, although the organization will probably go to some lengths to conceal its trade secrets or financial condition, your curiosity may turn up proprietary knowledge that you are not entitled to or lead you to ask questions you shouldn't ask. The reverse is also true: you should not volunteer information or answer questions that reveal proprietary knowledge about your last employer. In either case, the interviewer is likely to rate you low in integrity.

You may be justly proud of your educational achievements; but this can be one of the triggers in your interviewer's mine field. Keep in mind that the interviewer may not have had your educational opportunities and may be sensitive about it. If you seem smug about your schools, degrees, and honors, you may gain a point or two on education but lose several on interpersonal skills.

Secretiveness

Many years ago I interviewed a candidate who had nearly all the skills needed for a technical position in manufacturing. In person, he seemed an analytical, experienced individual. He gave specific examples of work experience on projects very much like the job he was being considered for.

Two items of information he did not volunteer were how much he had made in his last job and why he had left it. Because the employer wanted me to explore these topics, I asked the candidate the standard questions, but I couldn't seem to get any specifics from him. He was very skillful at deflecting the queries. He said, "I'm in the high-average range for my salary and years of experience in this type of work." His reason for quitting was "an unavoidable personality conflict which did not involve me, but the politics finally impacted on my job." Although this candidate seemed very principled and technically capable, the way he handled these legitimate questions suggested that he might be very rigid and uncompromising. The employer did not offer him the job.

Humor

Since good rapport can involve smiles, friendliness, and even laughter, it's easy to see how having a good sense of humor can help you communicate with the interviewer. However, some candidates try to project so much of their personality through humor that they forget the limits of good taste. Jokes that involve race, gender, national origin, religion, age, or disabilities are out of bounds; if you're tempted to tell a story with any of the above elements, stop yourself. Not only does such misuse of stereotypes reflect on your sensitivity and character, you may tread heavily on unseen toes without knowing it. Sacrifice your moment of humor for the dignity of others—and to stay out of a very hazardous part of the mine field.

A more constructive way to use humor is to take the edge off what might otherwise seem to be self-aggrandizement. One candidate I remember vividly described himself as a "clean, team machine." This earned him a smile from interviewers while getting across a succinct message about some of his strengths. In unfortunate contrast was another candidate's self-appraisal: "Smoking hot and packed tight, like Texas weed on a Saturday night!" Creative, all right, but the references to smoking, drug use, and frivolous entertainment did not serve him well.

Overtalking

It is possible to be too eager to communicate. I once asked a candidate a simple question, "What is your strong point?" and was inundated with a forty-five-minute list of his strengths—nine in all—with multiple examples of how he had used them in his former job. I tried several times to switch topics, but he persisted. I was unable to learn much of what I needed to know about him.

Most interviewers will see overtalking as self-indulgence or an attempt to control the interview. You should be alert to the interviewer's subtle clues and respond to his specific needs for information. If your answers are too long and too detailed, the interviewer may, at best, think you cannot distinguish the important from the trivial; at worst, label you a "motor mouth."

Money

Whether you're rich or poor, you have much to lose and little to gain in talking about money. The interviewer is likely to entertain such thoughts as these:

- "He doesn't have to work."
- "Spoiled rich kid!"
- "If he's so broke, how did he buy that sports car?"
- "She's probably poor because she ignored her education."

Even if the interviewer reacts positively to the saga of your fortunes, it probably won't do much to land you the job. What's important is not what you have or don't have, but what you can do for the organization. Astute managers know that the best workers are those searching for job enrichment and job satisfaction, not money. Communicate your driving need for work that is stimulating and exciting, and don't talk about salary until later.

Names

"It's not what you know, it's who you know." Don't you believe it. With few exceptions, employers are more interested in hiring people who can help them compete in the cutthroat marketplace than in running a corporate country club. Trying to gain an edge by dropping names will make most interviewers think, Can't this guy make it on merit? Claiming to know top executives in the organization may even be perceived as a threat.

One candidate I interviewed let me know in a not terribly subtle way that he was on a first-name basis with the governor of Tennessee. I was less than impressed; I had voted for his opponent.

Eating

Many interviews, especially those with candidates on the short list, are conducted over dinner. Managers sometimes simply like to dine out at company expense, of course; but don't assume that what you say and how you behave are off the record. Although the interviewer may tell you that she simply wants to get to know you better, be assured that she has specific objectives to cover during dinner. She may want to see how you conduct yourself in a more relaxed situation, whether you know the difference between consommé and a finger-bowl, how well you hold your liquor.

Table manners are a large part of the mine field; people grow up with different ideas of what constitutes good dining etiquette. Over the years I have seen good candidates sink themselves by carrying on lively conversations with mouths running over with food, using knives and forks like weapons, sampling food from other peoples' plates, obsessively separating a plate of food into

MANNERISMS THAT KILL RAPPORT!

Do you know your rapport-killing mannerisms? Of course you do. They're the ones your parents, teachers, and significant others have been pointing out to you for years. The problem is not your lack of awareness, it's the way you rationalize your bad manners: "This is acceptable in Europe," or "Well, it's just mashed potatoes, and there's no ash tray. . . ."

The following exercise should convince you that you need to make some improvements in this area. Ask someone—a person you trust to tell you the truth—whether she has ever seen you exhibit the following mannerisms. For those observed, ask whether the mannerism might hurt your image in an interview.

	Observed		Image	
	Yes	No	Negative	Positive
Playing with hair	❏	❏	❏	❏
Biting nails	❏	❏	❏	❏
Coughing	❏	❏	❏	❏
Sneezing without a tissue	❏	❏	❏	❏
Avoiding eye contact	❏	❏	❏	❏
Snapping fingers	❏	❏	❏	❏
Slouching	❏	❏	❏	❏
Tongue thrusting	❏	❏	❏	❏
Popping knuckles	❏	❏	❏	❏
Licking lips	❏	❏	❏	❏
Snorting	❏	❏	❏	❏
Cleaning fingernails	❏	❏	❏	❏
Picking nose	❏	❏	❏	❏
Pointing authoritatively	❏	❏	❏	❏
Clenching teeth	❏	❏	❏	❏
Wringing hands	❏	❏	❏	❏
Putting hands to face	❏	❏	❏	❏
Crossed arms	❏	❏	❏	❏
Tapping pen	❏	❏	❏	❏
Picking at face	❏	❏	❏	❏
Playing with keys	❏	❏	❏	❏

NEGATIVE VERBAL HABITS

Review the following list with someone who will tell you the truth. Ask whether he has ever heard you use any of the mannerisms, and whether the ones you are guilty of could hurt your image in an interview.

	Observed		Image	
	Yes	No	Negative	Positive
Mouth noises	❏	❏	❏	❏
Speaking too loudly	❏	❏	❏	❏
Speaking too quietly	❏	❏	❏	❏
Interrupting the interviewer	❏	❏	❏	❏
Stammering	❏	❏	❏	❏
Speaking too slowly	❏	❏	❏	❏
Too much irrelevant talk	❏	❏	❏	❏
Using profanity	❏	❏	❏	❏
Asking rapid-fire questions	❏	❏	❏	❏
Poor grammar	❏	❏	❏	❏
Using esoteric words	❏	❏	❏	❏
Thick accent	❏	❏	❏	❏
Mumbling	❏	❏	❏	❏

individual sections, and stirring everything together into an unrecognizable heap, gesturing wildly with utensils, and, of course, spilling their drinks into various laps. An interview over a meal provides hundreds of ways to get yourself evaluated on your eating habits rather than your skills.

Speech

Have you ever heard yourself on a tape recording and failed to recognize your own voice? This is a common experience, and an eye-opener. You hear yourself as others hear you. You thought you were being articulate, but now you sound overeducated. Slur a word, and you're illiterate. Speak slowly, and you're a yokel; fast, and you're a con artist.

Here, in my opinion, is a firm rule: Never use profanity. Now, you and I both know executives and others who habitually swear to emphasize a point; "It builds energy," they say. I am more impressed by people whose command of the language can convey a message without profanity. An interviewer who hears you swear is likely to think one of two things about your vocabulary: either it is inadequate, or it is offensive. The trend today is toward more profane public language; resist it.

There is one other current movement that you should, however, pay particular attention to: nonsexist language. Don't describe people exclusively with male pronouns; it insults half of the human race. Some men shrug this off as trivial. Many women disagree. Recently I interviewed a trainer who had programmed himself always to use both masculine and feminine pronouns when saying such things as "If the manager discovers an integrity problem, he or she should take immediate action." I gave him extra points for that.

SUSTAINING RAPPORT

If you have surmounted the wall and established rapport with the interviewer, then avoided the mine fields and maintained rapport, all that's left is to leave with good feelings high and without tripping over anything. You'll know when the end is near; the interviewer says something like, "Well, Jane, it looks like . . ." or moves into "What's gonna happen next" topics, or simply stands up and offers a handshake. This is your cue that you should prepare to exit stage left.

Things have gone well; don't push it. Limit your questions and comments to these topics:

- Your understanding of the next step in the process
- A statement that you really want this job
- A "thank you" for the interview

That's it! Smile and leave the room as gracefully as possible.

THE RAP ON RAPPORT

It's hard to get the toothpaste back into the tube, and it's almost as hard to overcome a bad first impression. I remember one applicant who disparaged a manager in his current organization, then, realizing that this made him sound judgmental, tried to recover by explaining that his versatility had enabled him to work well with the manager. Unfortunately, this comment only made him seem insincere. He dug himself in deeper during the rest of the interview by referring again and again to himself as a sincere, cooperative person who could work with just about anybody. Having made the original mistake, he compounded it by bringing the interviewer's attention to it.

Rapport is a two-way street, a measure of the good will and communication between you and the interviewer. There is a more overt side to establishing and maintaining a good feel in the interview—a side that is your responsibility alone. As the next chapter will show, your attitude going in is reflected in the way you appear and behave, and it can easily make the difference between acceptance and outright rejection.

CHAPTER 14

MIND YOUR
MANNERS

There's bad manners, and then there's bad manners.

There's the kind of bad manners where you know better, but you're so off balance because you've gotten an interview that you go for self-expression over humility. Or your life is in such disarray that the interview becomes a confessional and you end up sobbing on the interviewer's shoulder.

A good many otherwise qualified job candidates have lost out on job opportunities this way. I've heard a few stories and could tell a few myself: the highly qualified candidate, interviewing for a job in a very conservative organization, who repeatedly used foul language; the one who yelled at a receptionist; the one who complained about tight shoes while rubbing her bare feet. They should have known better. You, of course, would never make this kind of mistake. Not many do.

But a lot of candidates make the other mistake: bad manners due to ignorance. Every interviewer, every organization has unwritten rules of etiquette that you probably won't know in time to stop yourself from saying or doing the wrong

THE BASIC INGREDIENTS OF EFFECTIVE IMAGE

- Superficial components of image can help or hurt your career.
- The most effective image is the one held by successful people in your field.
- One detail askew can cause image confusion.
- Don't look too good—look professional.
- Don't "dress for success," dress for acceptance.

thing. For example, you comment on the terrible art hanging in the lobby which, it turns out, was painted by the founder's son. You talk about being sexually harassed, unaware that the organization you're interviewing with is tied up in a sexual harassment lawsuit. There are scores of particular things that you won't know not to do or say until it's too late.

SHOW RESPECT

Since you can't know all the particulars in advance, the best way to begin to meet your prospective employer's standard of etiquette is to stay in the mainstream. Read the organization's annual report, prospectus, or mission statement for clues to this "unwritten" code of conduct. Network with friends and acquaintances to locate someone who works or has worked there. If you've already developed a good relationship with someone inside the organization— an advocate—don't hesitate to ask about any pitfalls that might not be obvious to an outsider.

Be conservative in your social rituals, speech, dress, and manners. Think of good manners as showing respect for the feelings and sensibilities of others. Address interviewers as Ms., Mr., or Dr. until invited to use first names— especially with a person of another race or culture. Stand when someone enters the room. Communicate clearly and with proper business English. Wait for the other person to offer to shake hands. Do all this as if it were your everyday custom; don't make it look like you're doing something special for the interviewer.

Perhaps you're the kind of person who feels a need to express individuality through language and dress. You're perfectly free to look and act as you wish, of course—but you may be working at cross-purposes with yourself. What do you hope to gain from the interview—recognition, or a job? If it's truly the latter, concentrate on communicating what you can do, not who you are. Don't lead the interviewer to believe that you won't fit in with the rest of the team at work.

THE MAVERICK IMAGE

I once heard an interviewer describe a candidate who was being considered for a high-tech position in a very conservative organization. Not only did the candidate show up without a tie, he sported a ponytail and wore sandals. When he walked into the room, everyone wondered what he had accomplished that allowed him to be such a nonconformist.

As it turned out, he possessed highly specialized technical knowledge that the organization needed badly. Because of his unique level of expertise and the overwhelming needs of the company, his eccentric self-presentation did not work against him.

Here is a checklist of achievements that, in most organizations, might entitle you to present a nonconformist image without hurting your chances of getting a job. If you can check yes beside any of these statements, consider yourself free to develop whatever image you want.

Yes   No

❏   ❏   I received a Nobel prize.

❏   ❏   I am the principal contributor on a hundred or more patents.

❏   ❏   I was an effective and well-liked President of the United States.

❏   ❏   I am a world expert on a billion-dollar technology.

❏   ❏   I brought lasting peace to the Middle East.

❏   ❏   I invented ten-calorie beer.

If your credentials are so good that you can let self-expression dictate your image, you may have wasted your money buying this book. The rest of us should recognize that, however proud we are of our achievements, the only way we can get away with expressing ourselves in terms of odd clothing, extravagant jewelry, or devil-may-care grooming is to be the undisputed leader in our line of work.

But what about the particulars? Some can, fortunately, be defined in advance. Some topics and situations call for caution: certain personal preferences, legally protected topics, dining with interviewers, and many more. These we will deal with in more specific terms, because many a promising career has been thwarted by a seemingly trivial error.

TICKLISH TOPICS

Let's begin with the obvious. It's not the topics you're sensitive about that matter, it's those that bother the interviewer. You will naturally refrain from talking about things that make you feel uncomfortable. But you will not automatically avoid topics that distress others.

One day when I was teaching classes in sales fundamentals at the University of Memphis many years ago, we were discussing the importance of personal appearance in a sales presentation. One student, obviously noticing that I had adopted a "clean" haircut to obscure the fact that I was balding, boldly asked me how I felt about toupees. My immediate reaction was to answer with a jest: "I obviously think that a toupee would make a man look worse, not better!" The class responded with laughter—except for one student. He was the one wearing a toupee.

IMAGE CONFUSION

Image confusion occurs when one aspect of a person's image is not in line with the rest. Here are some examples:

- An executive vice president using a disposable pen to sign important documents
- A middle manager in a suit, with a ring in his nose
- An accountant wearing sandals
- A process engineer who wears a Rolex but drives a beat-up old car

Sometimes, of course, image confusion is the goal. Once, sitting in a downtown burger boutique, I saw two young men ride up on expensive Harleys. Their clothes were clean, their nails manicured—but both had dirty faces. On closer inspection, I saw that they had achieved their stylishly incongruous look with the help of makeup.

There's a television personality who once drove an old, beat-up Checker taxi. The car had a high-performance engine, lavish interior, fantastic stereo system—but car thieves didn't give it a second look. If it got dinged, that was okay. And not incidentally, it added a little creative dissonance to the person's image.

For your upcoming job interview, though, avoid projecting image confusion. Most interviewers are confused enough as it is. Strive for consistency.

My offhand response got a laugh and relieved some tension, but it also hurt, however momentarily, another person. Had I known that he wore a toupee, I might have thought of the injury my remark would cause in time to stop myself. With more wisdom and faster reflexes, I might have redirected the question to the class and let them deal with it. Instead, my joke probably took me down a notch in another person's eyes. Later I learned the general principle: Never talk about toupees around strangers.

Some topics are too risky even to mention in an interview. Almost nothing you say about them can help you, and just bringing up the subject can hurt you. The following five are the most dangerous.

Sex

Make no reference to sex. Specifically:

- Do not tell jokes with a sexual content.
- Do not make comments about sexual preference.
- Don't say anything about the sexual attractiveness of a person.
- Don't share sexual gossip.
- Don't comment on sexual problems, such as impotence.
- Don't talk about sexually transmitted diseases.
- Don't discuss how any form of life reproduces.
- Don't describe any advertisement that uses sex to sell a product.

Think of yourself as a person in a Norman Rockwell painting. There are, of course, differences in the way males and females dress, but beyond that there is no sex in the painting.

Gender Stereotypes

Old stereotypes of the roles of men and women are as outdated—and sensitive—in the workplace as in society at large. Most issues at work concern discrimination against women: unequal compensation, stereotypical job assignments, sexual harassment. There is a "glass ceiling" that keeps women from moving into positions of authority. Although progress has been made, these issues are still being worked out in many organizations. The employer you are interviewing with may have had painful experiences that the interviewer does not wish to be reminded of.

YEAH-BUT

I don't want to seem prudish. When I think the interviewer's joke is funny, I'm going to laugh, even if I'm ashamed of myself for laughing.

COACH'S COMEBACK

The way you respond to one interviewer may be overheard by another who considers the joke offensive. Simply don't react to off-color comments. You'll be amazed at how others will change their behavior to meet your higher standard.

Not all these issues are women's concerns. Some men complain about "male bashing," suggestions that they don't do their share of child care and household chores, and reverse discrimination. It's not wise to assume that all men like sports, are fascinated by cars, and prefer action movies. Many men are sensitive to the feelings of others and can color coordinate their clothing.

You may feel that you have at times been the victim of sex-based stereotyping and discrimination. You're probably right. In the interview, though, you're well advised not to comment on these issues, casually or otherwise.

Race

Any competent interviewer knows not to use race as a basis for either selecting or rejecting a candidate. However, some interviewers and some candidates think they can show how open-minded and flexible they are, or at least get the subject out of the way, by talking casually or making friendly jokes about race. This doesn't work well; simply bringing up the subject demonstrates that you have some concerns about it. Although there may be some exceptions, the best rule is not to mention race at all.

Here are some examples of things that you should not say:

- "I'm good at working with people of all races."
- "I am light skinned, but I still count as an African-American for your EEOC report."
- "I have no problem working with whites."

COACH'S TIP

Do yourself a favor: Don't say anything that reflects a stereotype about race, gender, color, religion, national orgin, age, disability, or sexual preference. Many interviewers view these topics as highly personal matters that are completely out of bounds in the interview.

- "When it comes to customers, I work best with other Hispanics."
- "Racism is alive and well in this country."
- "Since you're Korean too, tell me about my opportunities in this organization."

Some would suggest that you can intimidate an interviewer into giving you a higher rating by making a point of the fact that you are in a racial minority. I do not feel that this is a good tactic. It may instead make the interviewer look for legitimate reasons not to hire you. Forget race. Showcase your skills.

Social Standing

When talking to the interviewer about your skills, education, and job successes, you may find yourself edging into social standing, prestige, wealth, and contacts you know. Be very careful about this; such information may strike the interviewer as gratuitous bragging. I remember one candidate describing his close friendship with a well-known broadcast luminary—how often they met, which social events they attended. I was trying to learn what the candidate could do for the employer; he seemed more interested in saying, "Look who I know." A less objective interviewer might have seen him as a social climber, rather than the competent professional I found him to be. He got the job in spite of himself.

You need to use caution in talking about these topics:

- Your country club memberships
- How much money you have
- Famous people in your family
- Living at a prestigious address

- Driving an expensive car
- Always traveling first class
- Graduating from a prestigious university

This is not to say you should *never* talk about these things; just be cautious when you mention them. Social standing can work for you or against you—and sometimes both. I once participated in a series of interviews with a candidate who was being considered because he had graduated from the same top-name university as the CEO of the company. He mentioned his alma mater

CANDIDATE COMMENTS

Circle yes or no to indicate whether you believe the following comments are appropriate for a candidate to make. Compare your responses with the correct answers at the bottom of the next page.

1. Yes No "I am Italian."
2. Yes No "I have participated in six new-product rollouts."
3. Yes No "I'm a Christian."
4. Yes No "I'm taking a class in accounting."
5. Yes No "I know a lot about your biggest competitor's product plans."
6. Yes No "I always vote Republican."
7. Yes No "I developed the outplacement program my last employer used."
8. Yes No "I'm glad to see this organization has a policy on gay rights."
9. Yes No "I was the only woman in a department of forty-two men."
10. Yes No "I'm partially deaf, but I can do this job."
11. Yes No "She has a great figure!"
12. Yes No "I'm sixty-four, so you can use my age for your personnel reports."
13. Yes No "I was educated in London."
14. Yes No "I believe in not polluting the environment."
15. Yes No "My last boss was a nut."
16. Yes No "I am cured of cancer."
17. Yes No "I'm an alcoholic. I've been sober for three years."
18. Yes No "I have three children."
19. Yes No "My father-in-law just won the lottery."
20. Yes No "My hobby is hang gliding."

twice in an interview with line managers—most of whom had attended state colleges. They rated him intelligent, but not a good fit for the organization.

Confidential Information

Many organizations consider certain information confidential: trade secrets, proprietary technology, financial secrets, and so forth. Vendors and job candidates are sometimes asked to sign agreements not to disclose any such information they might acquire while visiting. If you seem too inquisitive, the interviewer may become suspicious of your intentions.

Suppose you are being interviewed for a government position that would give you access to protected information about nuclear weapons. If you ask questions, you must be careful to distinguish between public domain information and confidential information. The most practical guideline is not to ask for information that could not be published.

You should also use caution in asking about the organization's financial condition. You have a right to know whether the fiscal health of the organization might affect your long-term employment. On the other hand, "insider" information is off limits. This is often a judgment call, and asking the wrong question may not only raise suspicions but reveal your ignorance of the job you're applying for.

You should never expose confidential information regarding a current or former employer. To do so would be to break a confidence, which is unethical. The interviewer may take your willingness to share such information as a sign that you are not to be trusted, especially if you appear to be using it as a bargaining chip.

One other point: Suppose your interview is interrupted by a ringing telephone. Should you sit quietly until the interviewer is off the phone? No, etiquette suggests that you offer to leave the room to avoid overhearing a conversation the interviewer may consider private.

NO FREE LUNCH

In an article I read recently, two businessmen told how they used lunch to find out what they wanted to know about a candidate's personal life: "When we take

Key: Yes on 2, 4, 7, 10, 13; no on the rest.

DANGER ZONES

Notwithstanding all the guidelines you may be given, you must use your best judgment and your sense of the interviewer's interests, values, and experiences in deciding which topics you may safely bring up in an interview. The following, however, are especially likely to get you into trouble. Be careful what you say about

- money, because it may remind interviewers of their own financial problems.
- social causes, because the interviewer's opinions may be opposed to yours.
- politics, because the interviewer may vote differently.
- ethnic groups, because you may inadvertently insult the interviewer's relatives.
- age, because the interviewer may feel sensitive about getting older.
- disabilities, because you may be talking about someone the interviewer knows or is close to.
- gossip, because you unknowingly may be talking about the interviewer's personal problems.
- alcohol, because the interviewer may have a drinking problem.
- offbeat hobbies, because the interviewer may think that you are strange.
- religion, because the interviewer may be a fundamentalist or an atheist.
- sports, because the interviewer may hate your team.
- name dropping, because the interviewer may not like your famous friend.
- name blasting, because the interviewer may be a friend of your enemy.
- health, because the interviewer may be battling his own health problems.
- schools, because the interviewer may have gone to a rival school.

a female candidate to lunch, my partner and I begin talking with each other about our families—how old our kids are and what kinds of activities they participate in. After a while, the candidate wants to join the conversation. That's when we find about her child-care arrangements and whether she can really commit to doing the job."

This way of thinking is commonplace. A casual lunch conversation that you may assume to be off the record may well be staged to discover personal things about you. There is no free lunch.

Another problem with mealtime interviews is that people have different, and often strong, preferences about food, table manners, and dinner conversation, and these personal attitudes often conflict with business rituals. An old friend of mine was once invited to dinner by a group of Asian prospects who were considering a business arrangement with his company. To show their great esteem, they served him a specially prepared soup made with fish eyeballs. He was aware that his reaction was critical to their evaluation of him. "I knew that the customs were different," he said. "I also knew what I was in for when I was invited to dinner. I did what was necessary to accept their hospitality."

I once had lunch with a client and one of his candidates, a friendly but professional person who had performed well in the interview. Upon being told we were going to Pappy and Jimmy's Lobster Shack, he grew excited and exclaimed that he had always wanted to eat at "Pappy's." At lunch, his professional demeanor gave way to an apparent obsession with the food. He attacked a bowl of clam chowder the way Sherman took Georgia, then finished his entrée in five minutes. Instead of using the time to sell his job skills, he rhapsodized about every morsel of food.

Later, in spite of my arguments that the candidate was well qualified, he was turned down. A free lunch should not be allowed to interfere with a promising career, but it can.

FROM THE HORSE'S MOUTH, AND MORE . . .

As you can see, many of the things that can get you into trouble can be identified because they are true of most people and most organizations. There are others, however, that you may be able to discover by networking. If you know fifty people you can ask about your prospective employer, one or two of them may be able to tell you something, or to steer you to someone else who knows about the organization or has worked there or knows somebody who . . . and so forth. In other words, using your contacts can keep you within five or six connections of millions of others, some of whom can help you anticipate the organization's norms and social expectations.

Of course, the most important single device that can determine whether you are seen as a cultivated, considerate candidate or a buffoonish boor is your mouth. The next chapter will explore how hoof-in-mouth disease can sink an otherwise attractive job seeker.

CHAPTER 15

WATCH YOUR
MOUTH

In a one-hour selection interview, you will probably utter between five and ten thousand words; in a typical three-interview series, as many as thirty thousand. Now, here's something to give you pause: If you say 29,999 right words and one wrong one, you might as well have used your time standing on your head reciting the *Bhagavad Gita*.

Words are the essence of communication—and miscommunication. The interview begins; you're nervous. You're not as eloquent as you were in your fantasy interview, and you say something you don't mean. You leave out a key word and tell the interviewer exactly the opposite of what you intended. But . . . you can do worse.

To emphasize a point, you use the word "damn." The interviewer is offended. He decides that, if you cannot express your ideas without using profanity, your communication skills must be inadequate. But . . . you can do worse.

You hate the job you have now, and you spend most of the interview talking about how your crooked boss has mismanaged the company, and how you intend to file a grievance and possibly a lawsuit. The interviewer decides you're a troublemaker with poor teamwork and conflict resolution skills. But . . . you can do worse.

You're not sure you did well, and you'd like to get some feedback from the interviewer. But instead of simply asking him whether he found your responses helpful and suitable, you ask for suggestions on improving your interviewing skills. He infers that you're just using this interview as a practice session and have no intention of taking the job. But . . . you can do worse.

Your personal life is not going well, and you can't help mentioning that you're in financial trouble because your ex-spouse maxed out your credit cards on a cross-country trip with a new lover. You hope the interviewer can sympathize. The interviewer does not. You can do worse . . . but it's hard to say how.

THE RAPPORT TRAP

A good interviewer can make it easy for you to say the wrong thing. By building an easy rapport, he can lead you to feel comfortable talking casually about sensitive matters, as if he were an old friend. And if he's a very good interviewer, he won't let a slip of the tongue hurt your chances badly if you show competence in job-related areas.

But not all interviewers are this dispassionate, and not all the self-defeating things you can say in the interview are mere slips of the tongue. Some candidates drop their guard completely and let their feelings override their common sense. I remember one candidate, a police officer, who spent much of the interview venting his disgust with his fellow officers, the chief, and the entire department. He had an uncontrollable need to talk about how he felt, rather than taking the opportunity to sell his skills. I felt sorry for him, and for his wife and children.

Some candidates mistake the interviewer's friendliness for sympathy. One candidate I interviewed kept talking about his upcoming divorce and arguments with his wife—things I didn't need to know and that had no relevance to the job. I began to realize that he wasn't just blowing off steam; he wanted me to sympathize with him. Any good interviewer would realize that not only this

> ### COACH'S TIP
>
> If you are of one race and your interviewer is of another, you may be tempted to explain that you are not biased. This is a mistake. Don't mention race at all. Avoid showing that you noticed a racial difference. Focus your attention on the job rather than on the ways that you differ from the interviewer.

man's work but his relationships with his fellow workers were likely to suffer because of his personal problems.

Never take advantage of the interviewer's willingness to listen by turning the interview into a counseling session. Control the impulse to talk about all the things that get your goat. Don't rant about liberals, right-wingers, environmentalists, dog lovers, vegetarians. Don't tell the interviewer lurid tales of organizational deceit, bad politics, misuse of authority, or harassment. If you insist on volunteering such information, remember this: it will usually count against you. You will be branded a complainer.

Always remember that the purpose of the interview is to provide information about your fitness for the job, and that irrelevant information not only takes away from the time you have to sell your skills but may well count against you. Stay focused on the job, and keep the interviewer's attention directed to the excellent work you can do for the organization.

THE RELIEF TRAP

When you come to the end of the interview, whether or not you think it's gone well, you'll have a tendency to let down your guard. The ordeal is nearly finished; the die is cast; for better or for worse, you feel, there's not much you can do now to change the outcome.

And therein lies the trap. One interviewer told me that he had been interviewing a well-qualified engineer and was ready to offer him a job. Then he casually asked the engineer a simple question: "What would you do if you didn't get this job?" Without hesitation the engineer replied, "I'd sell my house, move to Colorado, and be a fishing guide."

Immediately the interviewer had doubts about the candidate's commitment to his career. The engineer was called in for more interviews, but eventually went away without a job offer. He had let down his guard and expressed his until-then well-hidden desire to drop out. The momentary loss of control had cost him what was probably his best job prospect.

I don't mean to say that you shouldn't dream. Of course you should. Dreams are healthy, and when pursued purposefully, they often lead to a fulfilling life and career. But when you're being interviewed, remember that your goal is to get offered the position you're interviewing for. Think about each question before you open your mouth—especially those innocent little questions that come out of nowhere after you think you've bagged the job.

WISH I HADN'T SAID THAT

In reviewing the notes I took in the course of several hundred interviews, I was surprised to see how many candidates made comments that worked against them. To some extent, it's understandable; the interview can be an emotional experience, and it's easy to blurt out something you later wish you hadn't said.

But many candidates go into the interview not knowing that they shouldn't talk about the intimate details of their personal lives, rancorous disagreements with their former bosses, insecurity about their careers. Part of your preparation should be to review things that you might be inclined to say but shouldn't. That's why I'm using the rest of this chapter to show you what a lot of people said that they shouldn't have said.

I have paraphrased these quotes, changing details here and there to avoid any possible disclosure of the candidate's identity, but preserving the speaker's meaning. You may find some of them offensive, but I'm taking that risk to make you think: What might I say in all innocence that others might find offensive?

What We Have Here Is Failure to Communicate

"I disliked working with that overbearing, egotistical a—. Everything was always my fault. I ignored him and did the best job I could."

"My boss told me I was too nosy. I just turned and walked away. I pondered it a long time."

"We had a sales blitz. One person seemed to undermine it. I was upset. I said to myself, Why am I busting it? So I set the record straight: I handled it head on with my boss."

"There was one operator who stunk. I talked to him, told him he had to take a bath."

How I Managed Not to Manage

"I chewed his a— out in front of all of them. I told him to get that look off his face or he could take a walk out the gate."

"He was noted for being a do-nothing. The work that had been required of him had been left undone. I stepped on his toes by doing all his jobs."

"I wander around 90 percent of the time in the office. I enjoy going to profit centers."

"I play fast-pitch softball. I'm a spikes-up type person, very aggressive."

"He seemed to think I was his key boy. . . . He gave me projects not related to my qualifications. I finally rebelled and said I can't do that."

"My nickname was Attila the Hun. I knew what my objectives were. . . . They respected me but I was disliked. . . . My staff said I was hard but fair."

"Some of my people were found smoking dope. I couldn't attack all the problems at once. I should have been more aggressive."

"My boss sees me as democratic. Some managers see me as autocratic— Vince Lombardi style."

"I like him. He's a maverick; he's got the spirit of a mustang, not blind obedience. I cut him slack I wouldn't cut anybody else."

"Better to have made a decision and be wrong than get the damn thing through a bureaucracy."

"My ability to look at all adverse consequences to a decision bites me in the butt sometimes. . . . If I had done a couple hours extra work, I would have gotten more facts."

"My boss says I'm about as subtle as a freight train."

Got Them Work-Habit Blues

"What do you mean, get results?"

"My number one interest is big-screen football."

"I work in spurts."

"Planning of what? I don't have to organize a plan."

"Screw me once, shame on you; screw me twice, shame on me."

"My work cycle used to be pretty radical: a short cycle every two months, a low that lasts for a week."

"I ruined five thousand dollars of equipment. I did exactly what my boss told me to do, even though I had reservations."

"I expect a lot from my superiors."

"I nibble all day in the deli. I'm sneaky. They caught me twice."

I've Got a Secret

"The company is paranoid as hell. They hired and fired eight people in three months."

"I found out a reformed alcoholic I liked was on drugs. . . . One time my boss's brother shot him. I took the statements and explained to my boss. It resulted in an arbitration. The brother was fired. I stuck by the man he shot."

"When I was working in a squad car, we picked up the vice president of XYZ, Inc. He was drunk, but instead of taking him to jail, we put him in a hotel room. We took his pants so he wouldn't leave the room."

"A lot of people don't like my boss. . . . A lady in another department had words with him and wanted to cry on my shoulder. I told her he just likes to agitate people."

Don't Hire Me, I Can't Cope

"I'm impatient. Incompetent people infuriate me. I get very upset, jump down people's throats. . . . I came down too strong on this one fellow, really reamed him out. I have a tendency to come on too strong."

"I had to let one of the office girls go. She had a very loud voice; she was rude. It took me several months to do it. I planned it. . . . I did it at a time that was convenient for me."

"You can't make nobody know nothing."

"I got so mad I had to walk off. My temper got me down."

"This one guy made me angry. . . . He had a lot on the ball, but had a habit of going to the office unnecessarily. . . . Other employees would notice. . . . He thought I was dumb. One time I caught him coming out of the office. I blew up. . . . I felt threatened."

"I thought he respected me. . . . He told me I was too immature. He thought my college education was a joke. I was crushed. . . . I was immature."

"I have a personality conflict with one of the vice presidents, I'm not sure why. . . . He drags me on the carpet for coming in fifteen minutes late three days in a row. During this time, the project manager had been out of the office for four days and was not reprimanded. . . . I kept working, but I wanted to punch his lights out."

"I'm very outspoken, and you know that can get you into trouble. . . . It's my temper. . . . I was short with my wife. She left home on me . . . sold her wedding ring for cash."

"As a police officer, I will not beat the hell out of someone for no reason at all."

More Than You Ever Wanted to Know, Period

"In a seminar, I met this guy. . . . I thought, Something's wrong here. . . . It turned out that he was trying to make love to my wife."

"My father and I were not friends."

"I used to have authority problems. . . . That's the reason I was in business for myself."

"I always hated my father as a child. . . . I later realized my mother was very ignorant, a small woman."

"I was a rebel. . . . In the military, I didn't like officers."

"I don't like to fail. . . . I don't have a lot of self-confidence."

"I require an extreme amount of stroking."

"I was losing perspective on my job. . . . I drank a lot. . . . The only thing that saved me was my people."

"I haven't been drunk in three years."

"I like the booze and parties pretty well . . . drinking heavily, chasing women."

"I was the class clown."

"I don't think I planned my life well enough. . . . I stumbled through a lot of things. . . . I should have finished school."

"My goal is to study my Bible more."

BENEFITING FROM THEIR MISTAKES

I asked several people to read these examples of interview self-destruction and give me their reactions. Here's some of what they told me:

"I was embarrassed for a person I don't even know."

"Some of these people didn't even have a clue!"

"I don't understand people who shoot their mouth off."

"I know the quotes are accurate, but I just can't believe that people would say things like this."

"People don't realize what they are saying."

The comments that seemed to create the most discussion were those that

- involved any form of profanity
- reflected little self-understanding
- indicated an autocratic management style
- showed deception or a lack of integrity
- depicted the individual as overconfident or lacking humility
- made any reference to religion

Many of the people who wounded themselves with the above comments got too comfortable and let down their guard. Another candidate, however, once said something that helped explain why so many people say things they shouldn't:

"When I was in the military, I would sit in the bar just to see what people talked about—you know, loose lips sink ships. I found that a moment of self-importance would cause other people to tell me things they shouldn't."

A good interviewer will make you comfortable, perhaps even self-important. You may be tempted to say what you shouldn't. This should raise alarms in your head. When rapport is high, think before you speak.

SELF-ASSESSMENT: SAYING THE WRONG THING

Review the SHARE answers you developed back in chapter 7, then ask yourself the following questions. Answer them aloud, as you would with an interviewer; you might tape-record them or practice in a small group with others who are preparing for interviews. Then evaluate each of your answers.

To what extent might your answer seem to indicate the following?

	1 Very Little	2 Little	3 Some	4 Great	5 Extreme
1. Willingness to use profanity	❏	❏	❏	❏	❏
2. Little self-understanding	❏	❏	❏	❏	❏
3. Autocratic management style	❏	❏	❏	❏	❏
4. Indecisiveness	❏	❏	❏	❏	❏
5. Tendency to make snap judgments	❏	❏	❏	❏	❏
6. Problems in coping	❏	❏	❏	❏	❏
7. Willingness to be deceptive	❏	❏	❏	❏	❏
8. Lack of integrity	❏	❏	❏	❏	❏
9. Overconfidence	❏	❏	❏	❏	❏
10. Uncooperativeness	❏	❏	❏	❏	❏
11. Lack of teamwork skills	❏	❏	❏	❏	❏
12. Failure to follow procedures	❏	❏	❏	❏	❏
13. Slow thinking	❏	❏	❏	❏	❏
14. Low work commitment	❏	❏	❏	❏	❏
15. Religious commitment or disbelief	❏	❏	❏	❏	❏

The poet Robert Burns once wrote the ancient Scottish equivalent of these words: .

> Oh, would some power the giftie give us
> to see ourselves as others see us.

There is valuable advice to be derived from this sentiment. Before you say what you were just about to utter, hesitate for a split second. Look at yourself from the other person's point of view. Watch yourself from afar, and hear yourself say what you are thinking of saying. How does it look? How does it sound? Is it a mistake? Is it a terrible mistake? Then don't say it. Curb your tongue. As American writer Elbert Green Hubbard once said, it is better to keep silent and be thought a fool than to speak and forever remove all doubt.

THE SHRINK WRAP

If you're like most of us, you'll come away from even a good interview with a vague feeling that you may have said the wrong thing once or twice. That's not something to get too concerned about. Nobody's perfect, and most interviewers discount the occasional slip of the tongue as meaningless.

Therefore, you shouldn't take it to heart if the interviewer asks you to meet the company psychologist. It's not a comment on your sanity, nor is it an illegal invasion of your privacy; it's the organization's way of evaluating whether you're likely to fit and work well within the organization, and it's a good sign that you're being seriously considered for the position. It's also the subject of the next chapter.

CHAPTER 16

MEET THE

SHRINK

You've been through several interviews with the organization, you've presented yourself and your qualifications well, you've built good rapport. Things are looking up. You think you might get offered the job.

Then they send you to the corporate psychologist.

What did you do wrong? Was it something you said? Was wanting this job a sign of insanity? You picture yourself lying on a leather couch, spilling your childhood secrets, while a frowning Sigmund Freud, cigar ashes on his beard, rocks in his high-backed chair and scribbles in his note pad. You fear that some hideous flaw in your unconscious will leap from your mouth and Freud will arch his eyebrow and the men with the butterfly nets will burst into the room.

Or worse, you might not get the job.

THE CORPORATE PSYCHOLOGIST

Being interviewed by the corporate psychologist can be the most terrifying part of the screening process. It's not like a regular interview, where you know most of the right answers. With a psychologist, your answers may tell more about you than you realize or want to reveal. You may feel your privacy is being invaded.

I am one of those corporate psychologists you worry about. Over twenty years I evaluated some five thousand candidates for a wide variety of jobs. I met many uniquely qualified individuals who worried about what I would do, how I would do it, whether they could handle the tests, what dark secrets I would discover in the depths of their psyches.

Now I am going to reveal what's behind all those mysterious assessments and tests. And you will see that it is not really so terrifying or dangerous after all. If you're prepared, and if you're the kind of person who will do well in the position to be filled, the psychological assessment will help you get in the right position.

WHY ARE ASSESSMENTS DONE?

It's natural to wonder why an organization would send you to see a psychologist as part of its screening process. There are many good reasons, ranging from life-or-death concerns to a natural interest in hiring well-adjusted individuals who will work together effectively. It's not that you're being singled out because you're an outsider, either. Many organizations hire or retain psychologists to guide their employees' personal and career growth, resolve conflicts between individuals or factions, prevent minor problems from becoming major ones, and in general monitor and modify working conditions to help individuals and the organization function more smoothly.

Legal requirements. Workers whose job performance could have public safety consequences are usually evaluated psychologically before being hired, and often at intervals during their careers. Many states require all law enforcement officers who carry a weapon to be assessed at employment to determine whether they are legally sane. Federal regulations require complete psychological assessments for all nuclear power plant employees, including vendors who service equipment on site. Major airlines assess pilots to see how well they react under stress in emergencies. More and more publicly licensed facilities, such as day-care centers and nursing homes, must now hire only workers who are known to be stable individuals.

Ultracompetitive selection. When many well-qualified people apply for a few jobs that require extensive knowledge and intensive training, a psychological assessment often decides the final selection. Astronauts, for example, complete regular performance and psychological evaluations throughout their careers. Those whose psychological functioning is questionable are sidelined or not allowed into the program.

Personnel audit. As an aid to long-range succession planning, some organizations assess not only prospective but current employees. Everyone in a particular job family is evaluated, then everyone being hired into the department. The objective is to describe the intellect, skills, and motivation of each person in a given job category, information that can be used to make decisions about promotions, training, and placement.

WHAT IT'S LIKE TO BE ASSESSED

The person who conducts your assessment will probably have had graduate training in the behavioral sciences, special course work in psychometrics, and supervised experience in individual assessment. However, this individual may not necessarily be a licensed psychologist; a well-trained assessor with an appropriate educational background can conduct interviews and tests designed by industrial organizational psychologists or other psychological specialists.

You will probably be evaluated using one of two standard procedures: the individual assessment or the assessment center. In a typical individual assessment, a psychologist spends a day interviewing you and administering tests to evaluate your suitability for the job. The day begins with a brief meeting, followed by four to six hours of testing. At some point the psychologist interviews you, using a structured interview designed to elicit information about your psychological functioning and work habits. Some assessors prefer not to test you but to rely on the interview alone. After the assessment, the psychologist reports to a contact within the organization, then follows up with a written report of the interview and test results.

An assessment center, unlike an individual assessment, typically brings together several candidates to complete exercises individually and as teams. Although designed by psychologists, an assessment center may be conducted by trained assessors, who observe candidates' behavior and compare notes on various performance dimensions. In a typical exercise, your behavior and suitability for the job may be evaluated based on competencies, such as those discussed in chapter 8, that the organization considers important.

Before the assessment begins, you will be told how the information will be used and who will have access to it. For promotion or selection, this usually means the organization only; your assessment will not be released to any other organization or person without your permission. In any case, the organization paying for the assessment generally treats your results as proprietary information.

If you are applying to go to work for the organization, you will probably not be granted access to the results. This privilege is usually reserved for internal promotion candidates or other internal assessments. However, if you end up getting the job, you may receive feedback to help you in your individual

DO I HAVE TO BE COMPLETELY HONEST ON THE PERSONALITY TESTS?

When you take a personality test, you will naturally wish to present yourself as positively as you can; you may be tempted to distort the truth. But psychologists are familiar with this natural tendency and have constructed tests to compensate for this self-bias. You're not likely to outsmart a well-designed test.

Consider the following multiple-choice question:

I would like to be_____.
  a. a poet
  b. an airline pilot
  c. a restaurant owner

When you read the question, you might say to yourself, "I'd really like to be a poet, but I don't want to sound like a wimp, so I'll say I'd rather own a restaurant." However, your guess about how each answer might be interpreted is probably wrong. "Poet" might score you high on creativity, while "restaurant owner" might get you a high mark on entrepreneurship, and "pilot" could mark you as adventurous. None of the interpretations involve any suggestion of weakness.

professional and personal development—not from a manager, but from a trained professional who can interpret your results.

STANDARD TECHNIQUES

Many different theories have been used in psychological assessments, and new ideas are continually being introduced into the field. In selecting people to fill jobs, however, organizations use primarily three types of assessment: personality-based, behavioral-based, and cognitive-based. You will complete standard tests, designed by a test publisher, on printed forms.

Standard assessment techniques do *not* include such things as dream analysis, word association, voice stress tests, handwriting analysis, or the use of colors for personality assessment. A few well-trained professionals in the past have used ink-blot tests, but that practice is so questionable that it is rare today.

Some tests control the tendency for self-promotion with forced-choice questions:

I am more _____.
    a.   irritating
    b.   hostile

Here the items reflect equally undesirable characteristics. Because you must respond to each question, you have to say some negative things about yourself. This makes it hard for you to distort your test results.

Personality measures often include honesty scales based on negatives that all people share:

Sometimes I am angry with people.
    a.   True
    b.   False

If you answer "true," you are admitting that you are like most people, because most people sometimes get angry with others. "False" may indicate that you're not very realistic about your possible negatives, or still worse, that you're trying to distort your test scores. Your overall profile can be statistically adjusted, based on your responses to these key questions, to counteract any attempt to skew your test results.

Although you can, of course, influence your test results by answering dishonestly, the results will be unpredictable, and it is unlikely that you can improve your assessment by doing so.

EXAMPLES OF PERSONALITY-BASED INTERVIEW QUESTIONS

1. What critical event in your childhood has most influenced your managerial style?
2. Which of your parents are you most like and how does your choice relate to your strengths and weaknesses at work?
3. Tell me what your biggest fears are on the job.
4. When it comes to stress, how can you tell when you're reaching your breaking point?
5. Are you more tough-minded or tender-minded, and why?
6. Are you more spontaneous and intuitive, or more sequential and linear in problem solving?
7. Tell me what the word "loyalty" means to you and explain how it relates to you as a person.

Personality-Based Assessment

The rationale behind personality-based assessment is that personality traits predict job performance. In order for this approach to be effective, the assessor must be highly trained, usually having a Ph.D. in psychology. Or the approach may involve the use of special formulas to carry out the prediction, without the input of a psychologist. These approaches involve tests and statistical procedures that use personality test scores to predict job performance. Accurate assessment of these traits often involves tests available only to professionals trained in their use. Formulas developed for specific jobs give the psychologist a statistical likelihood that a specific candidate will perform well.

Behavioral-Based Assessments

I feel that behavioral-based assessment is more straightforward than the personality-based approach. Responses to questions require little interpretation; job performance predictions are based on past behavior, not on statistical evaluation of test scores.

In this type of assessment, you may be asked to respond to two types of questions: behavioral-based or situational. Behavioral-based questions, as I explained in chapter 3, are phrased to elicit information about how well you performed in a past job action:

EXAMPLES OF BEHAVIORAL-BASED
INTERVIEW QUESTIONS

1. Tell me about a time when you managed conflict effectively.
2. Describe a situation in which you were able to effectively tell your boss some very bad news.
3. Showcase your teamwork skills by describing a team problem that you were able to resolve.
4. Give me an example of a way that you were able to organize yourself on your last job.
5. Describe a mistake you made in the last six months, tell me what you learned from it, then give me an example of how you used your learning.
6. Can you think of a time when you used common sense to justify breaking an important rule at work?
7. When have you been most guilty of being lazy on the job?

"Tell me about a time when you worked hard to get results."

"Describe an incident in which you failed to communicate as effectively as you could have."

The assessor uses your responses—that is, samples of your past behavior—to determine your behavior pattern and predict your future behavior.

Biographical information. Although behavioral-based assessment relies heavily on the interview, you may also be asked to complete various tests and questionnaires, such as the biographical information blank (BIB). Originally patterned after an application blank, the BIB is a life-history questionnaire designed to predict your future job performance based on how your background compares with that of previous successful employees—your education, job longevity, whether you grew up on a farm, and so forth. Your responses are used to derive a quantitative score based on such factors. This approach, elaborated over many years, has emerged as a highly effective selection instrument for specific jobs.

A typical biographical information blank might include fifty or more questions such as these:

1. What number best reflects the size of the town you lived in before you were twelve?
    a.   Under 5,000
    b.   Between 5,001 and 25,000
    c.   Between 25,001 and 100,000
    d.   Between 100,001 and 1,000,000
    e.   Over 1,000,000

2. At what age did you first earn money?
    a.   Before 5
    b.   Between 5 and 8
    c.   Between 8 and 10
    d.   Between 10 and 12
    e.   Between 12 and 16
    f.   Between 16 and 20
    g.   Over 20

3. What best describes the level of encouragement you received about your education before you were 20 years old?
    a.   Attend high school
    b.   Graduate from high school
    c.   Attend college
    d.   Graduate from college
    e.   Earn a master's degree or a doctorate

EXAMPLES OF SITUATIONAL INTERVIEW QUESTIONS

1. "Assume that you are working in a warehouse that contains valuable computer equipment. You work alongside a good friend who helped you get your job. What would you do if you saw your friend stealing company property?"

2. "You just came out of management training, where you learned how critical it is to follow procedures in your job, but now you are assigned to a manager who likes to do things intuitively. What would you do if your manager gave you a direct order that was inconsistent with procedures?"

3. "You're working on the third shift. Your spouse and children are sick with colds, and you're starting to feel symptoms. Your shift starts in three hours. What do you do?"

4. "Imagine that you are running a cutting machine that is a critical part of the production process. It is the only machine that can do what needs to be done to meet an extremely important customer order. The machine is set up with an alarm system that will warn the operator when a dangerous malfunction is likely. However, in the last week the machine has been giving false alarms. What would you do if the warning siren went off on your machine?"

Situational questions. In a situational interview, you are asked hypothetical job-related questions:

"What would you do if a customer used foul language and screamed at you?"

This approach measures your intentions, rather than your past actions. It is nevertheless behavioral-based because it uses your current behavior—that is, your verbal behavior in the interview—as the basis for prediction. It is also job related because each question concerns actions you would take in a hypothetical work situation.

Cognitive-Based Assessment

Cognitive assessment is the measurement of intelligence. Employers who use this approach base predictions about your job performance on your skills in solving problems involving such things as vocabulary, comprehension, mathematics, spatial visualization, and memory.

A typical cognitive assessment procedure is a pencil-and-paper problem-solving test on which you must answer as many questions as you can, either within a specified time or at your own pace. If you have a physical disability that would put you at a disadvantage on a timed test, tell the administrator; an untimed test can usually be substituted.

It is very important to understand and follow the instructions exactly. Some of the questions will be easy for you, but you probably won't be able to answer all of them correctly, because these tests are designed to measure an extreme range of problem-solving abilities. Don't feel bad if you can't answer all the questions; not many people can.

If you are given a computer-based cognitive test, the display will give you instructions, present questions, time your responses, and compile the results. This ensures that the test is administered and scored the same for all candidates.

EXAMPLES OF COGNITIVE-BASED INTERVIEW QUESTIONS ▬▬▬▬

1. How many miles is it from the earth to the moon?
2. Name the four main food groups.
3. What does "façade" mean?
4. What is the square root of eighty-one?
5. What is the relationship between torque and inertia?
6. Explain what is meant by H_2O.
7. How many grains of sand would there be in a one-gallon container?

SHOULD I GUESS ON PROBLEM-SOLVING TESTS?

When taking ability tests you will probably be asked to solve verbal problems, which involve vocabulary and logical reasoning, and numerical problems in basic arithmetic and number sequences. If you'd like a preview of the kinds of questions you'll be asked to solve, pick up one of the many books on preparing for college entrance exams.

On some tests, you are penalized for wrong answers; on others, you are not. The instructions should tell you whether it's in your favor to try to guess answers you are unsure of. If necessary, ask the test administrator. If there's no penalty for wrong answers, respond with your best guess. If wrong answers count against you, skip the ones you aren't reasonably sure of.

For years stories have made the rounds that such tests have a secret pattern of correct responses—for example, that on every fourth question "a" is the right answer. I cannot imagine why any candidate would believe that test developers would build in such a pattern as a cue to help the test taker beat the system. Actually, they go to great lengths to avoid doing so; anyone who designed beatable tests would soon be found out and professionally discredited.

THE NEXT STAGE

The interview is over. Now the waiting begins. You're entering a stage in your candidacy when your fate rests largely in the hands of others.

This does not mean, however, that you cannot begin a new candidacy. If you're wise, you'll be pursuing every opportunity you can find and not depending on your top choice to come through for you.

Opportunities have a way of disguising themselves. Sometimes you discover that the job you thought you wanted is not that great, and the job offered by a smaller organization for less money turns out to be the chance to hit it big.

This can be the most productive time of all for you. If you keep exploring all your options and evaluating your progress, you stand a good chance of putting yourself in the right place at the right time.

PART FIVE

GET READY
FOR THE
NEXT
CHALLENGE

We devote one of our Behavioral Interviewing® class sections to discussing the interview experiences of class participants. Most talk about the ways that being interviewed made them nervous. One participant, however, described her encounter with an interviewer who turned the tables on her.

"That's right, the interviewer was more nervous than I was. He fiddled with his tie and squirmed in his seat.

He actually had sweaty palms. Sometimes his nervousness was comical, but after a while I realized it would work against me when it came time to evaluate my interview performance.

"I tried everything I could think of to help him relax. I actually began interviewing him, asking about his career and current job. Then I talked about one of my experiences that paralleled what he was saying. But he never seemed to really feel comfortable when interviewing me.

"After the interview was over, a lot of things ran through my mind. Were my qualifications stronger than his? Did I remind him of someone who didn't work out on the job? Could he feel uncomfortable around attractive women at work? Still worse, did he think I was an EEOC plant who was going to scrutinize everything he did in the interview?

"As it turned out, he did give me high ratings, and I eventually did receive a job offer. But it was an unusual experience. It taught me to not jump to negative conclusions just because the interviewer makes a bad first impression."

It's not an uncommon experience to feel that an interview has gone badly, only to discover later that the impression was false. The period immediately after the interview is often a time when your tension and anxiety rise and your fears of unemployment resurface. You've done all you can do, and now your fate is in the hands of others.

This may be the hardest part of the whole process, especially for people who are disposed to action and feel edgy when events are out of their control. But, as you will see, there is still much you can do to help your chances with the organization you have interviewed with. And there is much you need to do to keep your spirits up, your opportunities growing, and your priorities straight.

The two chapters in this final part of the book will show you how to use your post-interview time constructively. Chapter 17 will show you how your interviewers and others in the organization evaluate your suitability for the position, and how you can help your chances by anticipating some of the things they will talk about. Chapter 18 offers philosophical advice on what to do if you're not offered the job, and—perhaps equally important—what to do if you're offered the job but have second thoughts about taking it.

CHAPTER 17

BEHIND CLOSED DOORS

You've filled out all the forms, taken all the tests, talked with everyone you can get in touch with. You've been interviewed by everyone in the organization. Now what do you do?

In many ways, this is the toughest part of the process. You've done all you can—or so it seems—and now your fate rests in the hands of people who are talking about you behind your back. You wait, and you worry. What's happening behind those doors?

HOW DECISIONS GET MADE

As a facilitator in a personal growth laboratory designed to help participants improve their communication skills, I once watched a powerful exercise called the "fishbowl." Three people sat in a circle and discussed a problem they all faced at work. A second group of three silently watched the three "fish" and took notes on how effectively they communicated. After fifteen minutes, the observers and the fish swapped positions. The observers spent their time in the fishbowl talking about how the three people they had observed could communicate better. The people who were being discussed had to sit outside the bowl and hear how they were perceived by the observers. Fifteen minutes later they were back in the fishbowl, describing what they heard and saw the others do when they communicated. After two rounds, everyone participated in an open discussion; then all six participants dealt with the original work problem.

I have often thought of the fishbowl exercise while helping an interview team decide on a candidate. I always wondered what the candidate might say after watching this process. At times I would have been proud to have the candidate listen. In other cases, the candidate would surely have been shocked to see how poorly some interviewers used the information gained in the interview.

In my work with interview teams, I got to see for myself how unfair subjective impressions can be. In one team discussion of several candidates, one interviewer wanted to hire a candidate because he was a "good Joe" who would fit in well with the existing work team. I considered another candidate better qualified; to hire the "good Joe" because of one interviewer's subjective reaction would be unfair to the other candidate. When I asked him for an interview example that would support his recommendation, his face got red, he raised his voice, and he shook his finger at me.

After this outburst, the selection team reviewed the qualifications of all candidates more objectively. Looking back on the experience, I like to think I was protecting a person from an arbitrary decision. But you may not be so lucky; there may be no one on the interview team who will argue for an objective decision.

Although your most active part in the process is over, you don't have to feel helpless. There's a lot you can do after the interview, while your potential employers are deliberating your fate, to improve your chances of getting a job offer. You can use the time constructively to increase your chances of getting a good job—whether this one or another. You can develop additional knowledge, skills, and abilities that will give you an edge over other qualified job candidates. And you can debrief yourself—that is, review your performance in the interviews, tests, and other parts of the process to see what you could do better next time.

COMMENTS MADE ABOUT CANDIDATES

In the meeting that follows your interview, subjective interviewers and objective interviewers usually have different things to say about your performance. The sample comments below suggest that you should use a positive-impression strategy with the subjective interviewer and an information strategy with the objective interviewer.

Subjective Comments

"She didn't appear to be career oriented."

"He's too good looking to work here. He'll distract the whole staff."

"It would seem strange with her driving the pumper truck."

"His belt didn't match his shoes."

"The customers won't respect her."

"He looks like an old hippie."

"I just don't feel she'll fit in with the team."

"He needs to lose about eighty pounds."

Objective Comments

"His skill with Spanish could pay off in the Texas market."

"She obviously has a broad range of programming experience."

"He doesn't have any sales experience."

"She graduated magna cum laude."

"He's accustomed to heavy travel."

"She's never worked in manufacturing."

"The facts suggest that he didn't cope very well with his last boss."

"She worked to pay for 80 percent of her college education."

CONSTRUCTIVE WAITING

The conventional wisdom says to write a follow-up letter after the interview to your primary contact reaffirming your interest in the job—and this time, the conventional wisdom is right. Now that you've been through the process, you know more about the organization than before. From the questions they asked, you know their interests, their concerns, their expectations. You know more about the job. Now you can follow through by offering additional information about your experience, skills, and abilities that can help them see you as the best candidate to fill the position.

It's also a good idea to monitor your progress through informal contacts with your advocate—or, if you haven't developed an advocate, the contact who arranged for your interview. Do so cautiously; sometimes the line between showing interest and appearing too eager is next to invisible. Remember that the interviewer has many other responsibilities, so don't make a pest of yourself.

Most candidates tend to be either optimistic or pessimistic about their chances of getting the job. Until you hear one way or the other, don't assume anything. One interviewer told me of a candidate with whom he had had great rapport and who had done very well in the interview. Unaware that he was competing with another highly qualified person and assuming that he would get the offer, the candidate quit his job to take some time off before starting the new job. He was shocked to discover that the position had gone to the other candidate. The interviewer was shocked that the candidate had made such an unwarranted assumption.

Sometimes you just don't know what to think. Maybe you're waiting to hear about your dream job, the kind of work you've spent years looking for and for which you think you'd be perfect. Because your hopes are so high, you find it hard to function normally. You wait for the phone to ring; you lose sleep; you worry. All this anxiety is wasted energy. If you get the job, you've worried unnecessarily, and if you don't, you've wasted time you could have spent productively.

The best way to spend your time after an interview is to keep looking for opportunities. This has many potential benefits:

- You turn your anxiety into productive energy.
- You will not appear overeager.
- You develop contacts to use if the job doesn't come through.
- You may find an even better job opportunity.
- You put yourself in a better negotiating position.

KEEP LOOKING!

One of my friends recently went through a particularly demanding job search. Here is what he told me:

"I was very aware that my job might be eliminated. I had a high salary, and my division was being acquired by a larger company whose existing staff could easily assume my job responsibilities. Nevertheless, I still felt a sting of anxiety when I was told I would be outplaced.

"There were special problems in my situation; the economy was bad, and for family reasons I felt I couldn't move. I also simply couldn't stand being out of work. I hadn't been out of a job since I was thirteen. I decided I wasn't going to be one of those guys who were still looking for a job three years after being outplaced. I'd go for the best job I could get, but I knew I'd be working, even if I had to drive a truck like I did in my early twenties.

"One of my first interviews was for my dream job—it was actually an advance over my last job. But while I was waiting for an offer, I continued to use my time to get other interviews. Although I felt confident about getting the job, I wanted to keep my options open. I worked twelve hours a day looking for new opportunities.

"I didn't get my dream job. But I wasn't dead in the water when I got the news. I used my momentum to network with venture capitalists. I got a three-month consulting job, which put me in line to replace a person who would retire in six months. I kept looking for interviews while I was consulting. But at the end of the consulting job I got an offer to stay full time.

"Paul, my advice to your readers is never stop looking while you're waiting for a job offer. It paid off for me. Some of the people who lost their jobs when I did aren't working yet."

TIE BREAKERS

Sooner or later the question arises, "What if it's between me and another candidate with similar qualifications?" How do interviewers make decisions with candidates who are equal? They use tie breakers.

Some tie breakers are best described as "value added"—characteristics, skills, or experiences that go beyond job requirements but offer added value to the organization. When you're competing for a job, value-added skills may tip the scales for the candidate with more to offer. Other tie breakers are more situational, such as how close you live to the job. Still others may simply reflect interviewer preferences—some of which may have merit, others of which may be questionable.

Breadth of skills. Candidates with a broad range of skills beyond job qualifications seem to have an advantage when decisions are close. For example, the CPA who also has a real estate license, the programmer who knows telephonics, the salesperson who can speak German—these candidates might be more attractive to the organization.

Geography. Where you live can work for you or against you, depending on the location of the job. The most obvious consideration for the employer is to avoid paying your moving costs. Of less significance is the distance you would have to commute. A candidate with a fifteen-minute commute could be more desirable than one with a ninety-minute commute. Also, your ability to access a major airport can be important, if you are being considered for a job that requires travel.

The previous job holder. If the last person failed in the job, any similarity between that person and you may work against you. The interviewer doesn't want to make the same mistake twice. Suppose you do well in the interview, but it turns out that you graduated from the same college as the last holder of the job. If it comes down to you and another equally qualified person, the organization, fearing that you will fail just like your predecessor, may hire your competitor. Unfortunately, there's not much you can do about this.

Diversity. Organizations that recognize the financial advantages of competing in diverse markets tend to place a high value on a diverse work force. Being a member of any protected category—gender, race, color, religion, national

COACH'S TIP

DON'T GET A LAWYER, GET A JOB

Now that you're past the interview and waiting for your potential employer to make a decision, you may think back and remember one or two questions that seem discriminatory to you. You may even have thought them illegal at the time and refrained from challenging the interviewer. If so, you probably made a wise decision, one that will rebound to your advantage.

You're in a good position. You have several possible courses of action: If you're offered the job, you can

- accept the offer and—on the assumption that the illegal questions represented only the interviewer's bias, not the organization's—go to work.

- decline the offer because you do not wish to work for an organization with such obvious bias against you.

On the other hand, if you do not get the offer, you can

- ask the company to reconsider because you feel the selection process was biased.

- bring legal action against the company for its discriminatory hiring practices.

- chalk it up to experience and be better prepared to respond the next time you feel you are subjected to biased questioning.

If you choose to bring legal action, you may have a good case, one that may eventually bring you a favorable settlement. Keep in mind, however, that you must balance your chances of winning against a large expenditure of money, aggravation, and time—time that might be used more productively in a career at another organization that will treat you more fairly.

origin, age, or disability—may give you the advantage if there is a close call between you and another candidate.

Employment fees. Some organizations place more confidence in candidates who have been screened by a search firm or a placement organization, and consider the costs of finding the right people minor compared with their potential productivity. Other organizations prefer to do their own recruiting. The only way to predict whether a recruiting firm will help or hurt your job chances is to know how the employer feels about paying others to screen their candidates.

Athletic skills. If the organization has sports activities, your athletic experience may figure in your chances of getting hired. One interviewer I heard of, hoping to win the league championship, hired a former college baseball player over other, more qualified candidates as a ringer on his company team.

Branch of military service. It's not unusual for former military people to prefer candidates who have served in the military—especially their branch of the service. If you were a marine and the interviewer was a marine, you have the inside track over an equally qualified ex-army candidate. An applicant with equivalent skills developed through civilian training may be shut out altogether.

Hobbies. Like other tie breakers, your hobbies can work for you or against you. Some, like hang gliding or collecting guns, may strike the interviewer as frivolous, expensive, strange, or dangerous. More helpful are hobbies linked with your career; an electrical engineer whose hobby is building computers is likely to gain tie-breaker points. Some employers want all your spare energy, and some candidates cater to that preference; as one executive told me, "Job first, family second. There's nothing left for hobbies."

Team experience. It used to be a factor in your favor if you played team sports; employers considered this evidence that you could work well with others. Team experience faded as a selection factor during the sixties and seventies, but has made a comeback because of the current emphasis on quality work teams. If you have had productive experiences in work teams, bring them out in the interview. If you haven't, indicate that you are adaptable to the needs of co-workers and customers.

DEBRIEFING YOURSELF

If you're the type of individual who learns quickly from experience, you'll recognize the interview as a very important and valuable learning experience. Now you have a little time to pause and reflect. What type of interview was it? Did you answer the questions as effectively as you could have? If you had it to do over, what would you do differently?

What you learn from the interview can be very helpful the next time you interview with another organization. Think of it as a data bank that you can draw on for your next project—getting a good job. But it can also pay dividends right away. In a close situation, when you and another candidate are similarly qualified and the company is not yet ready to decide, you may be called back for another interview. If you've thought about your last interview, you can give yourself an edge by adapting your approach.

Here's a key way to debrief yourself: Recall the kinds of questions the interviewer asked. Did the interviewer read questions from a form? It was a structured interview. Did the questions concern your personal thoughts and attitudes? You probably experienced a trait interview. With this fact in mind, review your trait profile from chapter 5 and evaluate how effective you were in giving examples that highlighted your positive traits.

The same is true of other interview styles. Questions about specific past job situations read from a form indicate a behavioral-based interview, the type of interview you've been preparing for if you've taken this book to heart. If you are interviewed again by this person or organization, be prepared to respond to queries with more SHARE examples and skill-benefit statements.

If the interviewer tried to put you at ease with a relaxed give-and-take dialogue, asking unwritten, apparently spontaneous questions that touched on your attitudes about work, that's the sign of a conversational interview. Review your self-definition in terms of your value profile from chapter 5 and emphasize your values in your answers.

An unstructured interview with questions coming out of left field, bearing no relation to your work experience, perhaps even verging on invasion of your privacy, is an indication of a gut-feel interview. It should lead you to reexamine the first impression you make upon people.

A SELF-INTERVIEW

After you've gone through an interview, ask yourself the following questions in order to learn from your experience.

Before the Interview
Did I:

- confirm my interview in writing or telephone?
- ask to pick up a job description?
- ask associates about the organization's culture?
- thank my advocate or contacts who helped me get the interview?
- review published company information?
- prepare my clothing ahead of time?
- arrive on time?
- check my grooming immediately prior to the interview?

Rapport Building
Did I:

- thank the interviewer for the interview?
- smile?
- avoid nervous gestures?
- correctly use the interviewer's name?

Start-Up Questions
Did I:

- get a descriptive question, like "What can you do for us?" If so, did I respond with a skill-based answer?

When the interviewers meet behind closed doors to discuss your interview performance, their decision will depend largely on whether their approach to the selection process is basically objective or subjective. Gut-feel and conversational interviewers will tend to focus on one or two of your responses—those they reacted to most strongly. With such interviewers—especially the gut-feel interviewer—you must be careful to avoid making the one comment that might kill your chances. Think back on the interview: Did the interviewer react strongly to anything you said? Did the rapport cool

- get a work-history question, like "Review your education and career for me"? If so, did I respond with an emphasis on the skills I learned and the achievements they were associated with?
- manage to use either script approach or the hero's journey to put magic in my career story?

Interviewer Style
- Was the interviewer more gut-feel, trait-oriented, conversational, or behavioral-based?
- What did I do to adapt to this interviewer's style?
- What types of skill-benefit statements did this interviewer seem most interested in?
- What mistakes did I make with this interviewer's style?
- What was the best answer that I gave in this interview?
- Did I seem natural in using my SHARE answers?
- What was a "killer" question that I had? How did I answer it? How do I evaluate my response?

Comments/Manners
- What did I say that may work against me in getting the offer?
- Did I say or do anything that might be inconsistent with this organization's culture?

Wrap-Up
- Did I get the interviewer's card?
- Did I ask about the next step in the process?
- Did I contact my advocate for feedback on the interview?

noticeably? Can you identify any factor that changed the feel of the interview? If you can, avoid that subject in any follow-up interview and in future job interviews.

Interviewers who use a structured approach, such as trait and behavioral-based interviewers, will compile and score your answers using standard methods before they discuss your interview performance. They are much less likely to let one or two of your responses keep you from getting the job.

THE DOORS SWING OPEN

After the organization has made its decision whether or not to hire you, you are faced with one further decision of your own: Will you accept their offer? Remember, it's a two-way street, and after experiencing a taste of your potential employer in the selection process, whether you are rejected or not, you may discover that the alternatives are not that bad—as we will discuss in the last chapter.

CHAPTER 18

THE ROAD
NOT TAKEN

In the summer after my junior year in college, I had a job at the Shelby County Penal Farm. All summer I took prisoners out to cut grass along county roads. One of them—a man the other prisoners called "Pigpen" because of his sloppy habits—was an expert in surviving prison life. I learned one of my most important life lessons from him, for Pigpen was very smart. He knew how to find work and make money, even in prison.

One day I saw Pigpen making what appeared to be a set of reins. I watched, puzzled. He attached them to the steering wheel of his mowing tractor. Then he started the tractor, put it in gear, lowered the blade, and began walking after it, tugging on the reins to guide it. "Just like plowing with a mule!" he said.

He had figured out a way to moonlight. While his tractor cut grass, Pigpen would walk behind it and collect bottles, worth a few cents each in deposits. At the end of the day he

249

would have ten dollars' worth of bottles. Day after day Pigpen's net worth grew. Among the prisoners, Pigpen was upper middle class.

Pigpen was an entrepreneur, an innovator, a go-getter. Although he didn't know it, he was an inspiration for me. Like any young person, I worried about not having enough money. Pigpen showed me my fears were groundless. If Pigpen could make a buck in prison, surely I could do as well on the outside, with an education and unlimited opportunity.

Since then, I have often thought of Pigpen. When I failed to get something I wanted, I would remember how Pigpen would live by his wits and cheerfully make do with what was at hand. It didn't take much money to make him happy. Surely I could do as well. No need to get upset; my skills would meet my basic needs. My disappointments were over things I wanted, not things I needed.

Recently someone in my Behavioral Interviewing® class was telling us how his last job had evaporated because his boss didn't like him. As he was describing his unhappiness in that job and how he felt he had been persecuted, suddenly something occurred to him. "You know," he said, "after I lost my job, none of the really important things changed. My health was good, my family was okay, and we paid our bills. The experience made me stay in touch with what was really important to me."

This is Pigpen's lesson to us all. As the Rolling Stones remind us, you can't always get what you want, but you may just get what you need. Sure, it's nice to be offered the job, to feel wanted; but fate may give you something you need instead. Keep this in mind when the option is yours. Your joy at being accepted may keep you from seeing that you'd be better off doing something else.

In many years of listening to people review their careers, I have found a common thread. When they hired on for meaningful work, they usually enjoyed their jobs and had good relationships with the people they worked with. When they took jobs for other reasons—location, money, status—they often ended up disliking their work and most of their co-workers.

ALTERNATIVE WORKSTYLES

When you are offered the job you so diligently sought, remember this: the final decision is yours. Do you really want to do the work? Are you well suited for it? Listen to your feelings. It may be a plum job with lots of money and prestige,

HOW BAD CAN AN INTERVIEW BE?

Here's a story told to me by a former job candidate who, after an apparently successful interview outcome, decided not to take the job.

"The interviewer leaned back in his chair, put his feet on the desk, and said, 'Tell me about yourself.' Right away, I felt I was wasting my time.

"I began telling him about myself, but soon found myself listening to his life history—where he went to school, his love of football, why he chose a career in sales, on and on through the first ten minutes of the interview. I guess he thought that by using this approach he was building rapport with me. Actually, he just seemed self-absorbed.

"When he was able to tear his attention away from himself, he asked me to describe my strong point. I told him I was organized. Then he asked about my weakest trait. I said that people told me I spent too much time at work. He seemed pleased with my weakness, even though my answer was obviously self-serving.

"He asked me about my job plans. As I was describing my career goals, his expression took on a wariness that made me think, This guy doesn't want anyone around who could get his job. I realized I had made a mistake: I had seemed too ambitious. Suddenly I was afraid I had killed my prospects.

"Toward the end, he began talking about his wife and family. I had the feeling he was trying to get me to talk about my personal life—but instead of revealing my private life, I asked him questions about his experiences at work. This seemed to make him like me more. He appeared not to realize I was interviewing him.

"Later they offered me the job. I turned it down. Who wants to work with someone so self-centered?"

---

but will you be happy? Just because you liked this kind of work in your last company doesn't mean that you'll like it in this one, where they do things differently and you don't know the people. In the everchanging workplace, the job you used to have probably doesn't exist anymore.

People still want meaningful work, but a career ladder seems to be a vanishing dream, tossed out with the excess layers of management that corporations are slicing away. Self-managed work teams and fewer supervisors are probably just around the corner for you, if you're not already there.

On the other hand, you may not want to do the kind of work you used to do. Like many others, you may prefer to redesign your work style to better accommodate your personal needs. Many bold spirits now go looking not for a job but for work that is spiritually fulfilling: "Life's too short to put up with what I used to have to do!" See if you can identify with any of the following people.

Urban Survival

Until about fifteen years ago, one acquaintance of mine worked for a major corporation. After deciding that he couldn't stand the politics and the stress of his job, he got a position in a government agency, but was invited to leave after two years. The recognition dawned on him that work in the traditional sense of the word was just not for him. He became what I call an urban survivalist, living off his ingenuity.

A college-educated man of average intelligence, more relaxed than driven, he was good with his hands and could live happily on next to nothing. He grew a garden behind his house for food. He didn't have to dress for work. He was out of debt. With time on his hands, he used some of his savings to divide his house into three apartments. The rental income paid his house note and gave him a little extra cash. He started doing odd jobs and carpentry. Over time he saved enough money to buy a second property, which he made into two apartments that increased his cash flow. He continued to do odd jobs and looked for deals to make extra money.

Today this man has over a million dollars in paid-for real estate and a healthy cash flow. He has been to Europe more times than I have and has more friends than a politician. Now he's talking about buying a shrimp boat and working and living on it for a while.

Look at him today and you see a person who is both personally and financially successful. And this happened because he chose never again to hold a traditional job. Just as farmers have been able to live on their land with a modest income, he has been able to live off of his apartments as an urban survivalist. He is happy.

Family First

I first met Thomas at a friend's party. He held a senior management position and a very bright future in a Memphis-based organization. He was smart, good looking, and capable. He was also facing the prospect of a move to Minneapolis because his employer closed out the local offices and required all senior management to work out of the corporate offices. Rather than move, Thomas accepted outplacement.

When I had the chance to talk with him later, he told me his reasons for staying put. He and his family loved their home; his children were doing well in school; he didn't feel that money was everything. I was surprised; I had never perceived him as a family-first man. But my perceptions were wrong. Thomas put his family above his career.

Thomas was very skilled at networking. He quickly lined up interviews, some with out-of-town employers who would let him live wherever he chose. Then came the dream job. It was in Chicago. It was so attractive that Thomas had to consider it. He and his family looked at condos in the city. He imagined what it would be like going to work every day in a limousine.

But Thomas turned down the job. He started a consulting company and now has several people working with him. He is financially successful. His family is happy. He is doing what he wants to do. When the job offers failed to match up with his wants, Thomas was able to say no.

Learn Your Way Out

Over the years I've had long-term consulting projects that enabled me to get to know the people in an organization very well. In one organization there was an extremely able professional, college educated and certified in her field. Her manager told me that she was going through a horrible divorce and facing severe financial problems. Her personal problems didn't affect her work, but they did make her question what she was going to do with her life.

One of the assignments in the time-management classes I was teaching was to set short-term and long-term goals. She said that her goal was to get a doctorate in English within six years. She wanted to do business writing and was especially interested in international business. Many of her goals were very specific: the money she would be making in ten years, the car and home she would own.

Soon thereafter, she enrolled in a graduate program. Offered an assistantship and a grant, she quit her job and earned her degree quickly. She has since returned to the organization in an entirely new role and has achieved her

A JOB DECISION INTERVIEW

The following structured self-interview is built around what I have found to be key factors in making an effective job decision. Many of them are issues that job candidates have raised when discussing mistakes they made in their careers, jobs they have taken when they shouldn't have, jobs they have turned down that would have been good for them. Ask yourself these questions, or have a friend interview you. Write down your answers and think about them. It will help you determine whether the job you want truly fits your needs.

Job Search

1. How effective and committed have you been in your job search? Are you pursuing your career goals systematically and with perseverance?
2. Have you contacted enough organizations to attain a good understanding of the value of your skills in the marketplace?
3. Have you prepared well for your interviews? Has a lack of preparation limited your ability to get job offers?
4. Have you been open to opportunities in organizations that do not have a well-known image?

Job Situation

1. Is the work to be done in a desirable location?
2. Are you satisfied with the compensation and benefits of the job?
3. Will this job situation be consistent with your family's needs?

---

professional goals. She had taken advantage of a personal disaster to move in an entirely new direction; education was both her escape and her road to higher goals.

Absolute Commitment

I have not been yelled at by many clients, but here's a story about a man who did just that. He was so committed to the idea of owning his own business that he wouldn't listen to reason. He had little cash and no experience in the line of business. I told him three times, as tactfully as I could, that the odds were very much against him. That's why he yelled at me. As it turned out, he was right and I was wrong. His blind commitment to his goal paid off.

4. Does this organization have a positive reputation? Will you feel proud telling people where you work?

5. Does this organization have products that are consistent with your beliefs? Do the products promote health, safety, and a clean environment?

6. Does this organization deal with people on their merits, rather than discriminating against them based on gender, race, color, national origin, religion, age, or disability?

Job Context

1. Will the culture of the organization fit your working style?

2. Does the organization have the fiscal ability and determination to protect your job? If not, are you willing to risk your career for the possible rewards?

3. Does this organization encourage you to express your opinions and participate in decision making, or is it autocratic, deciding issues from the top down?

Job Content

1. What aspects of the job may cause you to become dissatisfied with it? (Travel, entertainment, ambiguity, ethics)

2. Does this job fit your long-term career goals?

3. Will this job let you meet your own standards for honesty and integrity?

Before you think I am encouraging you to set unrealistic goals, let me tell you that this man was a very driven individual with a strong intellect. He had many useful personal assets: his family was behind him 100 percent, and he had more contacts than any two people. However, his biggest asset was his determination to own his own business.

By now you can guess how the story unfolds. He found a good business for sale and got on good terms with the owner, who wanted to retire. He financed his start-up with money from his retirement plan and a second mortgage on his home. He learned the business quickly and made it grow, and grow, and grow. I'm sure he's quite wealthy by now.

When he yelled at me, I thought he was out of control. I was wrong. He was and is very much in control of himself—both in work and in life. His high standards sent him in quest of work that he liked instead of just another job. This kind of commitment can be a lesson for us all.

The Death Dream

A close friend of mine quit his job in a major corporation after having what he called a "death dream":

"I woke up in the middle of the night in a cold sweat. I had dreamed that I was an old man, sitting at the same desk in the same office that I have now. My boss walked in, but he was now very old, too. He started his usual high-pressure game and even in my dream my stomach knotted up just like it does now at work.

"I was relieved that it was just a dream. But the horrible feeling lingered on until I realized that the dream was a warning about something very real that was happening to me. I was dying a slow death in my job. The only reason I went to work was to get money. The only friends I had at work were political communication channels. My enemies were ready to misconstrue anything I said and raise doubts about anything I did.

"My death dream told me that I had to leave my well-paid job in a highly respected organization. My greatest career risk was staying, not going."

My friend resigned on the day that he had fifteen years of tenure in the organization, the cutoff point for his long-term retirement benefits. He called his boss from a public phone in the Denver airport, explained that he was planning to leave, and offered to make the transition as painless as possible. His boss appreciated the gesture but suggested they could fill the job internally with no problems.

I recently spoke with this person. He has a new job in a new industry and says he's never been happier.

Each of these stories shows how you can use your innate wisdom and courage to find meaningful work. In each case the individual pursued a goal, stated or unstated, that combined personal desires with work opportunities—a work search, not a job search.

BUILDING BRIDGES BEHIND YOU

Here is some of the best advice I ever got: "Don't burn any bridges behind you. If things don't work out, you may have to work for that person again."

When you accept a job, remember everyone you talked with along the way. If you don't accept it, remember the people who took the time to assess your skills and recruit you for the position. And when you are rejected, say thank you for your time. Each of the people you talked with may be a gateway for new opportunities later on. At a minimum, keep business cards and phone lists handy for future job searches.

You may stay in touch with an interviewer with whom you've established good rapport. People I interviewed years ago call now and then just to stay in touch. One person I interviewed in 1978 sends me a card every year during the holiday season. I know, of course, that it's his way of saying, "Remember me." Still, I'm flattered that he considers me a valuable long-term professional contact.

In the larger scheme of things, doing well in your career takes more than just acing your interview. Winning strategies for getting your next job involve more than just showcasing your skills as you handle interview questions. The most important strategy of all is to be a real person, honest in your dealings with others, and willing to follow your passion in your work.

NOTES

Chapter 1

1. I have consciously focused this book on how a job candidate can honestly communicate what he or she can actually do for an employer. I have avoided giving ways to answer specific questions that may help you pass an interview. In particular, this book does not refer to the actual questions or skills that are presented to the clients of Behavioral Technology®, Inc., who are learning how to be better interviewers. This book is designed to help you educate yourself on how to structure your own honest answers. It will not coach you on how to fabricate answers to specific questions that you may be asked.

2. For more on this idea, read *JobShift*, by William Bridges (Reading, Pa.: Addison Wesley, 1994).

Chapter 2

1. Ibid.

2. See William B. Johnston and Arnold H. Packer, *Workforce 2000, Work and Workers for the 21st Century* (Indianapolis: Hudson Institute, Inc., 1987). More recent information on diversity may be found in U.S. Department of Labor, Bureau of Labor Statistics, *Occupational Outlook Quarterly*, Fall 1995; U.S. Department of Labor, Bureau of Labor Statistics, *Monthly Labor Review: The Work Force in 2005*, November 1995; and Anthony Carnevale and Susan Stone, *The American Mosaic* (New York: McGraw Hill, 1995).

3. U.S. Department of Labor, Bureau of Labor Statistics, "The American Work Force: 1994–2005." *Occupational Outlook Quarterly*, Fall 1995.

4. Tom Peters and Robert Waterman, *In Search of Excellence* (New York: Harper & Row, 1982).

5. Tom Peters, *Thriving on Chaos:* Handbook for a Management Revolution (New York: Harper & Row, 1989).

6. Tom Peters, *The Pursuit of WOW!* (New York: Vintage Books, 1994).

7. Michael Hammer and James Champy, *Reengineering the Corporation* (New York: Harper Collins, 1993). A good practical application of these

ideas can also be found in Harold S. Resnick's *Business Process Reengineering: An Executive Resource for Implementation* (Marlborough, Mass.: Work Systems Associates, 994).

8. Al Gore, *The Gore Report on Reinventing Government* (Washington D.C.: The Government Printing Office, 1993).

Chapter 3

1. For more information on the speed at which interviewers make decisions, see chapter 17. See also B. M. Springbett, "Factors Affecting the Final Decision in the Employment Interview" (*Canadian Journal of Psychology* 12, 13–22), and M. R. Buckley and R. W. Eder, "The First Impression" (*Personnel Administrator,* Spring 1988, 72–75). A more academic treatment of first impressions in the interview can be found in a study by Theresa Hoff Macan and Robert L. Dipboye, "The Relationship of Interviewer's Preinterview Impressions to Selection and Recruitment Outcomes" (*Personnel Psychology,* 1990, 43).

2. There are several different ways for an interviewer to learn the behavioral-based approach. Behavioral Technology®, Inc., of which I am the CEO, regularly offers public workshops on this topic across the United States and Canada. Our training video, *More Than a Gut Feeling,* provides a dramatic enactment of the Behavioral Interviewing® technique. For more information, call (800) 227-6855. A more academic presentation of the technique is found in Tom Janz, Lowell Hellervik, and David Gilmore's *Behavior Description Interviewing: New, Accurate, Cost Effective* (Toronto: Allyn and Bacon, Inc., 1986).

3. Situational and simulation interviews technically fall in the behavioral based category that I have described in the model of interview styles. However, I have not emphasized these types of questions in this book because you will encounter mostly past-event questions. Consequently, my reference to behavioral-based interviews refers to job-related, structure interviews that use singular, open-ended questions about past events.

The "What if . . ." approach of the situational interview is well researched and valid as an interviewing strategy. For a literature search on the situational interview, begin with Gary Latham and B. J. Finnegan,

"Perceived Practicality of Unstructured, Patterned, and Situational Interviews" in H. Schuler, J. L. Farr, and M. Smith (Eds.), *Personnel Selection and Assessment: Individual and Organizational Perspectives* (Hillsdale, New Jersey: Erlbaum, 1993), 41–55.

Chapter 5

1. The Secretary's Commission on Achieving Necessary Skills, *What Work Requires of Schools: A SCANS Report for America 2000*, U.S. Department of Labor, June 1991.

2. In our Behavioral Interviewing® classes, we train interviewers to use competencies (we call them "skill definitions") and related questions to develop structured interviews. In this book, it is my objective to help the reader prepare for a wide variety of interviews, not to coach a candidate on how to take a behavioral interview. Consequently, I have used the competencies originally designed in the SCANS project. These competencies are available to you through the text list in chapter 5, pp.75–78.

Chapter 7

1. There are times when an interviewer calls for answers that are very different from the SHARE example. Some of these questions are basic start-up questions, which we will deal with in chapter 9. In a simulation interview, you are asked to show what you can actually do—for example, a typing test. Be prepared to demonstrate your skills under the instructions of the interviewer. In a situational interview, you are asked to describe what you would do in a future, or hypothetical, situation. In this case, base your answer on a past experience that you would probably repeat.

Chapter 9

1. For more on this idea, see Syd Field, *Screenplay: The Foundations of Screenwriting* (New York: Dell, 1982).

2. I found two videos on the work of Joseph Campbell to be an excellent way to understand his thinking. See Bill Moyers, *Joseph Campbell and the Power of Myth, Program One: The Hero's Adventure* (New York: Mystic Fire Video Inc., n.d.) and *The Hero's Journey: The World of Joseph*

Campbell: Transformations of Myth Through Time (Public Media Video, 1987).

Chapter 13

1. See B. M. Springbett, "Factors Affecting the Final Decision in the Employment Interview" (*Canadian Journal of Psychology* 12, 13–22).

2. See M. R. Buckley and R. W. Eder, "The First Impression" (*Personnel Administrator,* Spring 1988, 72–75).

INDEX

For special orders and bulk purchases, or for more information on Behavioral Technology's interviewing and performance management products, call (toll free) **1-800-227-6855** or fax **901-763-3637.**

Quantity discounts are available.

Visa/MasterCard/American Express/Discover accepted

To order by mail, enclose check with your order payable to

Behavioral Technology®, Inc.
6260 Poplar Avenue
Memphis, TN 38119-4719

GET HIRED!
WINNING STRATEGIES TO ACE THE INTERVIEW
Hardcover . . . $24.95 / Paperback . . . $14.95

ABOUT BEHAVIORAL TECHNOLOGY®, INC.

For more than twenty-five years, Behavioral Technology®, Inc., headqu;
Memphis, Tennessee, has developed training and consulting pro;
selection and performance management. BTI's premier produ
Behavioral Interviewing® system, which has been implemented in Fo1
companies across the United States, Canada, and parts of Europe ;
Clients of Behavioral Technology, Inc., include Hewlett-Packard, I1:
Holiday Inn Worldwide, Polo Ralph Lauren, Purolator Courier Ltd
Express, Blue Cross/Blue Shield, Bell Mobility Canada, and Warner I

The Behavioral Interviewing process has been widely accepted
companies because of its practical approach to assessing a candid
related skills. Research has found that structured interviews with (
regarding job skills and past job actions enhance the reliability and \
the selection interview.

In addition to its Memphis headquarters, Behavioral Techn(
sales consultants in Atlanta, Chicago, Dallas, Denver, Sacramento,
ton, D.C., and in Vancouver and Montreal, Canada. For more inform
(800) 227-6855 and ask for your regional account executive.